U.S. and CANADA LITERATURE ORDER FORM

NAME: ______________________________

COMPANY: ______________________________

ADDRESS: ______________________________

CITY: ____________________ STATE: __________ ZIP: __________

COUNTRY: ______________________________

PHONE NO.: (   ) ______________________________

ORDER NO.	TITLE	QTY.		PRICE		TOTAL
			×		=	
			×		=	
			×		=	
			×		=	
			×		=	
			×		=	
			×		=	
			×		=	
			×		=	
			×		=	

Subtotal __________

Must Add Your Local Sales Tax __________

Postage: add 10% of subtotal → Postage __________

Total __________

Pay by check, money order, or include company purchase order with this form ($100 minimum). We also accept VISA, MasterCard or American Express. Make payment to Intel Literature Sales. Allow 2-4 weeks for delivery.

☐ VISA ☐ MasterCard ☐ American Express Expiration Date __________

Account No. ______________________________

Signature ______________________________

Mail To: Intel Literature Sales
P.O. Box 58130
Santa Clara, CA 95052-8130

International Customers outside the U.S. and Canada should use the International order form or contact their local Sales Office or Distributor.

For phone orders in the U.S. and Canada
Call Toll Free: (800) 548-4725

Prices good until 12/31/89.

Source HB

INTERNATIONAL LITERATURE ORDER FORM

NAME: ______________________________

COMPANY: ______________________________

ADDRESS: ______________________________

CITY: ____________________ STATE: __________ ZIP: __________

COUNTRY: ______________________________

PHONE NO.: (   ) ______________________________

ORDER NO.	TITLE	QTY.		PRICE		TOTAL
			×		=	
			×		=	
			×		=	
			×		=	
			×		=	
			×		=	
			×		=	
			×		=	
			×		=	
			×		=	

Subtotal __________

Must Add Your Local Sales Tax __________

Total __________

PAYMENT

Cheques should be made payable to your local Intel Sales Office (see inside back cover.)

Other forms of payment may be available in your country. Please contact the Literature Coordinator at your local Intel Sales Office for details.

The completed form should be marked to the attention of the LITERATURE COORDINATOR and returned to your local Intel Sales Office.

80960KB HARDWARE DESIGNER'S REFERENCE MANUAL

1989

Additional copies of this manual or other Intel literature may be obtained from:

Intel Corporation
Literature Sales
P.O. Box 58130
Santa Clara, CA 95052-8130

CG-051989

TABLE OF CONTENTS

CHAPTER 1
80960KB PROCESSOR ARCHITECTURE

1.1 Introduction 1-1
1.2 Architectural Attributes for Embedded Computing 1-1
1.2.1 Load/Store Design 1-1
1.2.2 Large General Purpose Register Sets 1-2
1.2.3 Small Number of Addressing Modes 1-3
1.2.4 Simplified Instruction Format 1-3
1.2.5 Overlapped Execution 1-4
1.2.6 Minimum Cycle Operation 1-4
1.3 Additional 80960KB Architectural Enchancements 1-4
1.3.1 Floating-point Operation 1-4
1.3.2 Debug Capablities 1-5
1.4 Standard Bus Interface 1-5
1.5 Inter-agent Communication/Co-processor Capabilities 1-5
1.6 Summary 1-5

CHAPTER 2
80960KB SYSTEM ARCHITECTURE

2.1 Overview of a Single Processor System Architecture 2-1
2.2 80960KB Processor and the L-Bus 2-1
2.3 Memory Module 2-2
2.4 I/O Module 2-3
2.5 Summary 2-3

CHAPTER 3
THE 80960KB AND THE LOCAL BUS

3.1 Overview of the 80960KB L-Bus 3-1
3.2 Basic L-Bus States 3-1
3.3 L-Bus Signal Groups 3-3
3.3.1 Address/Data 3-3
3.3.2 Control 3-4
3.4 L-Bus Transactions 3-7
3.4.1 Clock Signal 3-8
3.4.2 Basic Read 3-8
3.4.3 Write Transaction 3-9
3.4.4 Burst Transactions 3-11
3.5 Timing Generation 3-14
3.5.1 80960KB Processor Clock Requirements 3-15
3.5.2 Clock Generation 3-15
3.5.3 Open-Drain Pullups 3-17
3.6 Arbitration 3-17
3.6.1 Single 80960KB Processor on the L-Bus 3-18
3.6.2 State Diagram 3-18
3.6.3 Arbitration Timing 3-20
3.6.4 Two 80960KB Processors on the L-Bus 3-21

3.6.5 Bus States for Two 80960KB Processors 3-21
3.6.6 Arbitration Timing for Two 80960KB Processors 3-23
3.6.7 Bus Exchange Example Between Two 80960KB Processors 3-23
3.6.8 A Peripheral Device As the Default Bus Master 3-24
3.7 Inter-Agent Communication (IAC) 3-25
3.7.1 Overview of IAC Operations 3-26
3.7.2 IAC Messages 3-26
3.7.3 Hardware Requirements for External IAC Messages 3-27
3.7.4 Message Buffers 3-27
3.7.5 IAC Pin Logic 3-27
3.8 External Priority Register 3-28
3.8.1 Hardware Requirements 3-28
3.8.2 External Priority and IAC Messages 3-28
3.9 Interrupts 3-29
3.9.1 Interrupt Signals 3-29
3.9.2 Interrupt Control Register 3-30
3.9.3 Using the Four Direct Interrupt Pins 3-31
3.9.4 Using an External Controller 3-31
3.9.5 Using IAC Requests for Interrupts 3-33
3.9.6 Synchronization 3-33
3.9.7 Interrupt Flows 3-33
3.9.8 Pending Interrupts 3-34
3.9.9 Interrupt Latency 3-37
3.10 Reset and Initialization 3-40
3.10.2 RESET Timing Requirements 3-40
3.10.3 RESET Timing Generation 3-40
3.10.4 Initialization 3-41
3.11 Error Singals 3-44
3.12 80960KB Self-Test 3-45
3.12.1 Scope of Self-Test 3-45
3.12.2 Test Algorithm and Operation 3-45
3.13 Summary 3-46

CHAPTER 4
MEMORY INTERFACE
4.1 Basic Memory Interface 4-1
4.1.1 Data Transceivers 4-1
4.1.2 Address Latch/Demultiplexer 4-3
4.1.3 Address Decoder 4-4
4.1.4 Chip Select Generation 4-5
4.1.5 Burst Logic 4-6
4.1.6 Burst Ready Generation 4-8
4.1.7 Byte Enable Latch 4-9
4.1.8 Bus Command Generation 4-10
4.2 SRAM Interface 4-11
4.2.1 SRAM Interface Logic 4-11
4.2.2 SRAM Timing Considerations 4-11
4.3 DRAM Controller 4-15

4.3.1 Address Muliplexer 4-16
4.3.2 Refresh Interval Timer....4-17
4.3.3 Arbiter 4-17
4.3.4 DRAM Timing and Controller 4-17
4.3.5 Timing Considerations for the DRAM Controller 4-20
4.4 Summary 4-23

CHAPTER 5
I/O INTERFACE

5.1 Intefacing to 8-Bit and 16-Bit Peripherals 5-1
5.2 General System Interface 5-1
5.2.1 Data Transceivers 5-3
5.2.2 Address Latch/Demultiplexer 5-3
5.2.3 Address Decoder 5-3
5.2.4 Timing Control Logic 5-3
5.3 I/O Interface Design Examples 5-4
5.3.1 8259A Programmable Interrupt Controller 5-5
5.3.2 Interface 5-5
5.3.3 Operation 5-7
5.3.4 82530 Serial Communication Controller 5-7
5.3.5 82586 Local Area Network Co-processor Example 5-9
5.3.6 Interface 5-9
5.3.7 Operation 5-11
5.3.8 82786 Graphics Co-processor Example 5-11
5.3.9 Interface 5-12
5.3.10 Operation 5-15
5.4 Summary 5-15

Figures

1-1. Local Register Set....1-2
1-2. Global Register Set....1-3
2-1. Basic 80960KB System Configuration....2-2
3-1. Basic L-Bus States....3-2
3-2. L-Bus Signal Groups....3-3
3-3. Byte Enable Timing Diagram....3-5
3-4. Clock Relationships....3-8
3-5. 80960KB Processor Read Transaction....3-9
3-6. 80960KB Processor Write Transaction....3-11
3-7. Processor 2-word Burst Transaction....3-12
3-8. Processor 3-word Burst Read Transaction....3-13
3-9. Processor 4-word Burst Write Transaction....3-14
3-10. CLK2 Edges....3-15
3-11. Typical Clock Logic for 80960KB....3-16
3-12. L-Bus States Arbitration....3-19
3-13. Arbitration Timing Diagram for a Bus Master....3-20
3-14. Arbitration Connection between Two 80960KB Processors....3-20
3-15. L-Bus States for Secondary Bus Master....3-22
3-16. Arbitration Timing Diagram for an SBM....3-23
3-17. Example of a Bus Exchange Transaction....3-24
3-18. Forced Relinquishment Timing Diagram for an SBM....3-25
3-19. Example Flow Chart for an IAC Operation....3-26
3-20. IAC Response Data....3-28
3-21. Physical Address Range for IAC Messages....3-29
3-22. Interrupt Control Register....3-31
3-23. Timing Diagram for Interrupt Acknowledge Transaction....3-32
3-24. Flowchart 1....3-35
3-25. Flowchart 2....3-36
3-26. Flowchart 3....3-37
3-27. RESET Timing Diagram....3-40
3-28. Asynchronous RESET Circuit....3-40
3-29. Timing Diagram for RESET Generation....3-41
3-30. Initialization Flow Chart....3-42
3-31. RESET Signal Timing Relationship....3-43
3-32. Initialization Circuity....3-44
4-1. Simplified Block Diagram for Memory Interface Logic....4-2
4-2. Data Transceivers....4-3
4-3. Address Lactching....4-4
4-4. Input Control Circuity....4-5
4-5. Chip Select Logic....4-6
4-6. Burst Logic Flow Chart....4-7
4-7. Burst Ready Generator (BRG) Block Diagram....4-9
4-8. Logic Diagram for SRAM Interface....4-12
4-9. Critical Timing Path for SRAM Read Operation....4-13
4-10. Critical Timing Path for SRAM Write Transaction....4-15
4-11. DRAM Controller Block Diagram....4-16
4-12. Flow Chart for DRAM Timing and Control Logic....4-19

4-13. Timing Diagram for Two-word DRAM Read Transaction 4-22
4-14. Timing Digram for Two-word DRAM Write Transaction 4-23
5-1. Simplified I/O Interface................................5-2
5-2. I/O Timing Control Block Diagram................................5-4
5-3. Block Diagram for 8259A Interface................................5-6
5-4. Block Diagram for 82530 Interface 5-8
5-5. LAN Controller 5-10
5-6. Bloack Diagram for 82786 Interface 5-13
5-7. Operational Flow Diagram for 82786 Interface Circuit................................5-14

Tables

3-1. SIZE Signal Decoding................................3-4
3-2. Byte Enable Signal Decoding 3-5
3-3. Summary of L-Bus Signals 3-7
3-4. Combination of Bus Masters................................3-18
3-5. Interrupt Latencies 3-38
3-6. Constituent Parts of the Base Latency................................3-38
3-7. Special Case Latencies 3-39
4-1. Byte Enable Signal Decoding 4-10

Preface

PREFACE

This manual serves as the definitive hardware reference guide for system designs using the 80960KB processor. Hardware designers can use this manual as a guideline for developing microprocessor systems. Readers of this manual should be familiar with the operating principles of microprocessors and with the 80960KB datasheet.

NOTE

The information for the 80960KB processor also applies to the pin-compatible 80960KA version. The 80960KA processor implements all 80960KB functions except for floating-point operations.

This manual presents the 80960KB system design from a hardware perspective. Other information on the software architecture, instruction set, and programming of the 80960KB processor can be found in the *80960KB CPU Programmer's Reference Manual.*

Together with the *80960KB Hardware Designer's Reference Manual*, these publications provide a complete description of the 80960KB system for hardware and software designers.

MANUAL ORGANIZATION

The manual is divided into five chapters. These chapters describe how to build a hardware system using a single 80960KB processor.

- **Chapter 1.** Briefly introduces the 80960KB component architecture.
- **Chapter 2.** Presents an overview of the 80960KB hardware system design, which includes a system configuration illustrating the various components that constitute an 80960KB system.
- **Chapter 3.** Describes the local bus and the interface to the 80960KB processor. This chapter includes detailed signal descriptions and discusses timing generation, arbitration, interrupt handling, and initialization.
- **Chapter 4.** Discusses techniques for designing memory subsystems.
- **Chapter 5.** Presents guidelines on how to interface I/O devices to the local bus.

Introduction to the 80960KB Microprocessor

1

CHAPTER 1
80960KB PROCESSOR ARCHITECTURE

1.1 INTRODUCTION

The 80960KB is the first 32-bit microprocessor designed especially for embedded applications. At an operating frequency of 25 MHz, this high performance processor sustains an instruction execution rate of ten million instructions per second (MIPS), and burst rates of 25 MIPS.

The 80960KB processor integrates special features which enhance embedded system performance. These features eliminate the need for additional peripheral devices and associated software overhead. For example, the 80960KB processor offers an on-chip floating-point processing unit, an improved interrupt handling capability, and support for debugging and tracing.

This chapter describes the architectural attributes and enhancements of the 80960KB processor for embedded computing.

1.2 ARCHITECTURAL ATTRIBUTES FOR EMBEDDED COMPUTING

For over a decade, Intel has designed a large variety of 8- and 16-bit microcontrollers to fit the needs of embedded applications. Because the 80960KB processor incorporates the following attributes in its architecture, embedded applications are easy to design, perform well, and get to market fast.

- Simple load/store design
- Large general-purpose register sets
- Boolean and bit field instructions
- Small number of operations and addressing modes
- Simplified instruction format
- Minimum cycle operation

1.2.1 Load/Store Design

In the 80960 family architecture, operations are register-to-register, using only LOAD and STORE instructions to access memory. This attribute simplifies the instruction set and shortens cycle time. It provides a 512-byte, direct-mapped instruction cache to further minimize memory accesses. The processor performs burst transactions that access up to four data words with one-word transfers every clock cycle.

1.2.2 Large General Purpose Register Sets

Because the instructions operate on operands within registers, the 80960 family features a large, versatile register set. For maximum flexibility, each processor provides thirty-two 32-bit registers and four 80-bit floating point registers.

There are two types of general purpose registers: local and global. The processor automatically accesses the 16 local registers when it performs a procedure call. Figure 1-1 illustrates how the processor stores multiple sets of local registers on-chip to further increase the efficiency of this register set. The register cache holds up to four local register frames, which allows the processor to perform up to three procedure calls without the need to access the procedure stack resident in memory.

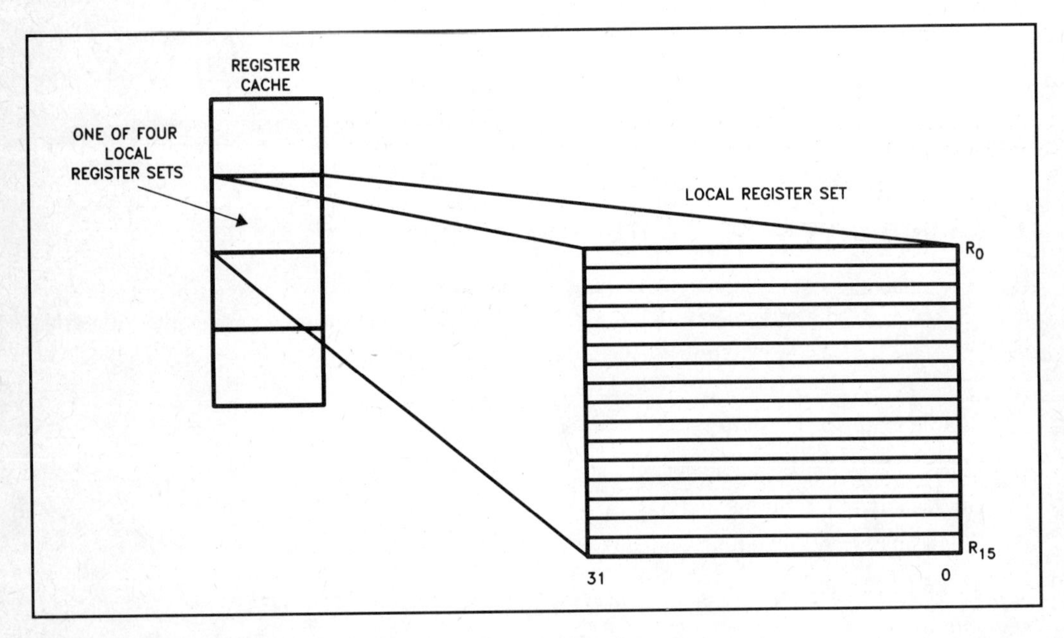

Figure 1-1: Local Register Set

The 20 global registers retain their contents across procedure boundaries. Figure 1-2 shows that the global registers consist of sixteen 32-bit registers (G_{15} through G_0) and four 80-bit registers (FP_3 through FP_0). While all registers can hold floating point operations, the programmer should use these 80-bit registers for accumulating extended precision results.

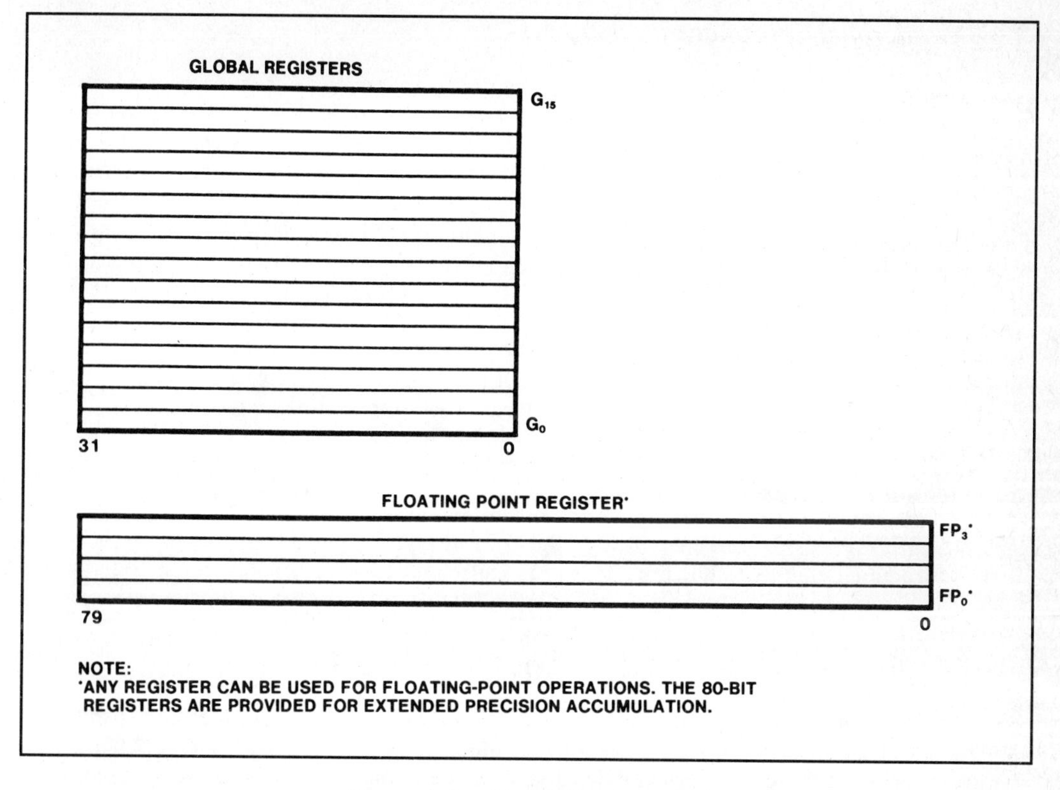

Figure 1-2: Global Register Set

1.2.3 Small Number of Addressing Modes

The 80960 family uses relatively few addressing modes. This allows the control engine to facilitate a fast, simple interpretation of the command set. In addition to fast addressing modes, the 80960KB processor also provides a few complex addressing modes to increase code density.

1.2.4 Simplified Instruction Format

A simplified instruction format eases the hardwired decoding of instructions, which also speeds control paths. The 80960KB processor's instruction formats are simple and word aligned; all instructions are one word long except for one class that uses the subsequent word as a 32-bit displacement. To further enhance performance, the instructions do not cross word boundaries. This feature eliminates a pipeline stage (needed to align instructions) and decreases instruction execution time.

1.2.5 Overlapped Execution

To optimize performance, the 80960KB processor employs write buffering and register scoreboarding to overlap instruction execution. Write buffering allows a write instruction to proceed as soon as the processor places it in the buffer. It does not need to wait for the actual write operation to occur on the L-bus.

Similarly, register scoreboarding is a design technique that allows the 80960KB to continue execution of instructions when it encounters a LOAD instruction. When the LOAD instruction begins, the 80960KB sets a scoreboard bit on the target register. After the target register receives data, the processor resets the bit. While the processor is retrieving data, it transparently (requiring no software) checks the scoreboard bit to ensure that these additional instructions never reference the target register. In this manner, the scoreboard feature reduces the effect of slow memory speed and provides a useful tool for optimizing procedures.

1.2.6 Minimum Cycle Operation

The 80960KB processor executes most of the core instructions in a single clock cycle. For these instructions, the 80960KB processor uses hardwired logic rather than microcode to execute the instruction.

The 80960KB also supports a number of important multicycle instructions (such as 32-bit multiply and divide instructions). These auxiliary functions require more than one clock cycle because it is more efficient to use microcode than hardwired logic. On the other hand, the integration of these functions on-chip eliminates much software overhead. The functions also eliminate the negative effects of code density. This additional functionality of the 80960KB enhances overall system performance while retaining small code size.

1.3 ADDITIONAL 80960KB ARCHITECTURAL ENHANCEMENTS

The 80960KB incorporates useful features such as on-chip floating-point processing, multiprocessing capabilities, and debugging functions that support breakpoint instructions (bit-tracing, branching, and others).

1.3.1 Floating-point Operation

The on-chip floating-point unit of each processor eliminates the bus overhead needed to transfer operands to a co-processor, thereby improving the performance of floating-point calculations. The processor also provides hardware support for both mandatory and recommended portions of IEEE standard 754 for floating-point arithmetic, exponential, logarithmic, and other transcendental functions. The 80960KB integrates the floating-point unit on-chip to reduce the overall chip count for a system, decrease power consumption, and increase overall performance and reliability.

1.3.2 Debug Capabilities

The processor provides extensive system debug capabilities, which helps speed software development. The 80960KB processor allows breakpoint instructions that stop program execution for various events such as procedure calls or certain instructions. Another debug facility traces the activity of the processor while it executes a program. Tracing records the addresses of instructions that cause trace events to occur. For example, a trace event occurs on the execution of a specific instruction, branch, or procedure call.

To ensure that the 80960KB is operating properly, the processor performs a self-test when it is reset. The self-test feature tests both the processor itself and the integrity of the memory system. If the self-test is successful, the 80960KB begins operation; otherwise, it enters the stopped state.

1.4 STANDARD BUS INTERFACE

Advanced features of the 80960KB processor implement a performance-optimized bus interface. The processor uses a high bandwidth local bus (L-bus) which consists of standard signal groups: a 32-bit multiplexed address/data path, and control signals for data transactions. Because of the large amount of cache, the L-bus supports burst transactions that transfer up to four successive data words. Transactions on the L-bus can use 8-, 16-, and 32-bit data types and address up to 4-Gigabytes of physical memory. The processor uses the hold request/hold acknowledge protocol to accomplish bus arbitration.

1.5 INTER-AGENT COMMUNICATION/CO-PROCESSOR CAPABILITIES

The 80960KB processor offers a flexible way to manage interrupts. It accepts interrupts in one of three ways:

1. Communicates with an external interrupt controller using the standard Interrupt/Interrupt Acknowledge signals
2. Activates the on-chip interrupt controller
3. Accepts an inter-agent communication (IAC) message. This allows the 80960KB to act as a co-processor on a shared bus with another CPU.

1.6 SUMMARY

The 80960KB processor uses a new 32-bit architecture to optimize embedded system performance. The family architecture includes a load/store design, large general purpose register sets, fast addressing modes, a simplified instruction format, and minimized instruction execution cycles.

To further enhance system performance, the 80960KB processor provides floating-point operation, interrupt controller capabilities, debug functions, and multiple processor capability. The 80960KB integrates these functions on-chip to reduce the power requirements and overall chip count for a system.

Because of the architecture, the 80960KB processor provides unprecedented performance. For a speed selection of 25 MHz, it can sustain an instruction execution rate of over ten million MIPS and burst rates of 25 MIPS, which is comparable to that of super-minicomputers. The high instruction execution rates are possible through an innovative design that incorporates an on-chip instruction cache with burst-transfer capability.

80960KB System Architecture

2

CHAPTER 2
80960KB SYSTEM ARCHITECTURE

This chapter illustrates the flexibility and power of the 80960KB system architecture using the advanced 32-bit 80960KB processor. It examines system configurations from a general perspective to explain design concepts. Subsequent chapters describe the details of system design.

2.1 OVERVIEW OF A SINGLE PROCESSOR SYSTEM ARCHITECTURE

The central processing module, memory module, and I/O module form the natural boundaries for the hardware system architecture. A high bandwidth 32-bit multiplexed L-bus connects the modules together. The L-bus can transfer data at a maximum sustained rate of 65.6 Megabytes per second for an 80960KB processor operating at 25 MHz.

Figure 2-1 shows a simplified block diagram of a typical system configuration. The heart of this system is the 80960KB processor, which fetches program instructions, executes code, manipulates stored information, and interacts with I/O devices. The high bandwidth L-bus connects the 80960KB processor to memory and I/O modules. The 80960KB processor stores system data, instructions, and programs in the memory module. The processor accesses various peripheral devices in the I/O module to directly support communication with other ancillary subsystems.

2.2 80960KB PROCESSOR AND THE L-BUS

The 80960KB processor performs bus operations using multiplexed address and data signals and provides all the necessary control signals. The processor provides Intel standard control signals, such as Address Latch Enable ($\overline{\text{ALE}}$), Address/Data Strobe ($\overline{\text{ADS}}$), Write/Read command (W/$\overline{\text{R}}$), Data Transmit/Receive (DT/$\overline{\text{R}}$), and Data enable ($\overline{\text{DEN}}$). The 80960KB processor also generates byte enable signals to specify which bytes on the 32-bit data lines are valid during the transfer.

The L-bus supports burst transactions, which access up to four data words at a maximum rate of one word per clock cycle. The 80960KB processor uses the two low-order address lines to indicate how many words to transfer. The processor performs burst transactions to load the on-chip 512-byte instruction cache to minimize memory accesses for instruction fetches. The processor also uses burst transactions for data access.

To transfer control of the bus to an external bus master, the 80960KB processor provides two arbitration signals: hold request (HOLD) and hold acknowledge (HLDA). After receiving HOLD, the processor asserts HLDA to grant control of the bus to an external bus master.

The 80960KB processor uses an on-chip interrupt controller or an external interrupt controller (or both) to provide a flexible interrupt structure. An internal interrupt vector register specifies the type of interrupt structure. For a system with multiple processors, another method is available, called inter-agent communication (IAC). This type of message allows one processor to interrupt another.

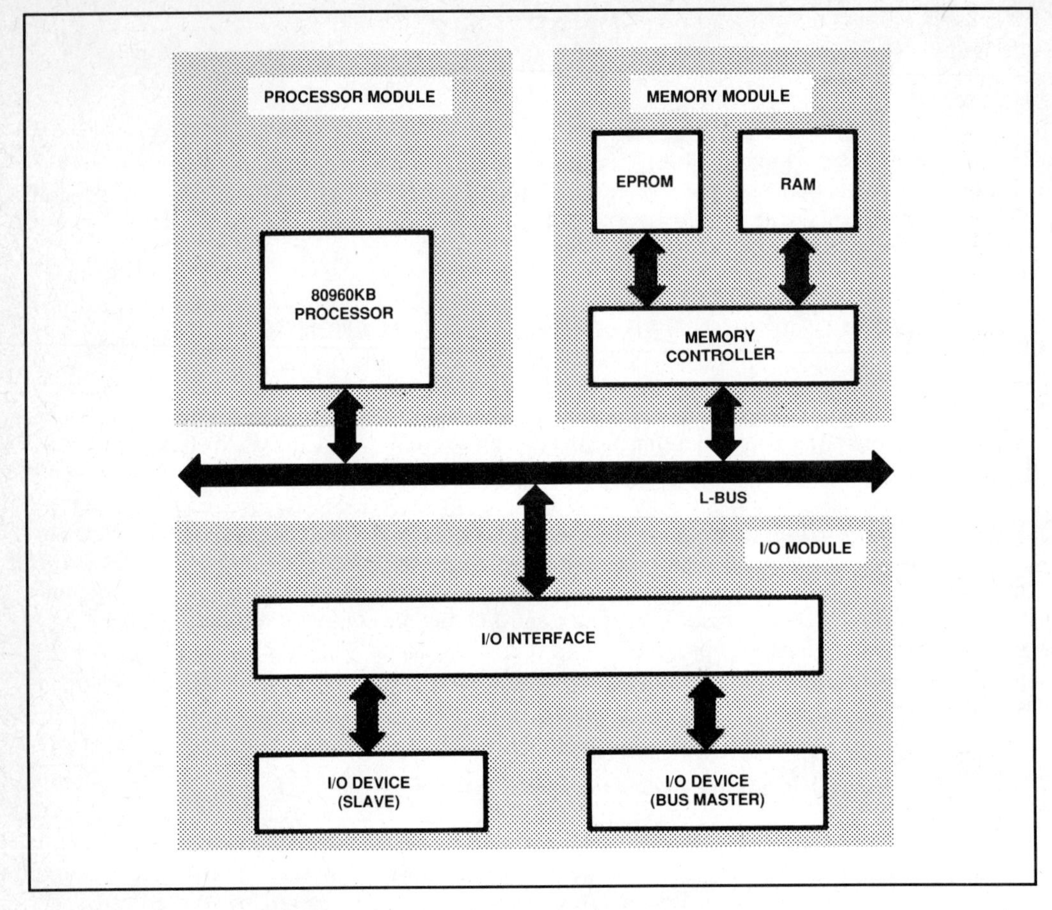

Figure 2-1: Basic 80960KB System Configuration

2.3 MEMORY MODULE

A memory module can consist of a memory controller, Erasable Programmable Read-Only Memory (EPROM), and static or dynamic Random Access Memory (SRAM or DRAM). The memory controller first conditions the L-bus signals for memory operation. It then demultiplexes the address and data lines, generates the chip select signals from the address, detects the start of the cycle for burst mode operation, and latches the byte enable signals.

The memory controller generates the control signals for EPROM, SRAM, and DRAM. In particular, it provides the control signals, the multiplexed row/column address signals, and the refresh control for dynamic RAMs. The controller uses the static column mode or nibble mode features of the dynamic RAM to accommodate the burst transaction of the 80960KB processor. In addition to supplying the operation signals, the controller generates the $\overline{\text{READY}}$ signal to indicate that data can transfer to or from the 80960KB processor.

The 80960KB processor directly addresses up to 4-Gigabytes of physical memory. To ease the design of the controller, the processor does not allow burst accesses to cross 16-byte boundaries. Each address specifies a four-byte data word within the block. The processor uses four byte enable signals to access individual data bytes.

2.4 I/O MODULE

The I/O module consists of the I/O components and an interface circuit. I/O components allow the 80960KB processor to use most of its clock cycles for computational and system management activities. Time consuming tasks can be off-loaded to specialized slave-type components, such as the 8259A Programmable Interrupt Controller. Other tasks may require a master-type component, such as the 82586 Local Area Network Control (LAN).

The interface circuit performs several functions. It demultiplexes the address and data lines, generates the chip select signals from the address, produces the I/O read or I/O write command from the processor's W/$\overline{\text{R}}$ signal, latches the byte enable signals, and generates the $\overline{\text{READY}}$ signal. Because these functions are the same as some functions of the memory controller, both interfaces use identical logic. For master-type peripherals that operate on a 16-bit data bus, the interface circuit translates the 32-bit data bus to a 16-bit data bus.

The 80960KB processor uses memory-mapped addresses to access I/O devices. This allows the CPU to use many of the same instructions to exchange information for both memory and peripheral devices. This allows the powerful memory-type instructions to perform 8-, 16-, and 32-bit data transfers.

Chapter 5 examines representative design examples to help describe design guidelines for the I/O interface.

2.5 SUMMARY

The basic hardware system configuration using the 80960KB processor is modular and flexible. The processor, memory, and I/O modules form the natural boundaries in the basic hardware system architecture. The high-bandwidth L-bus that supports burst transfers establishes the data path between the 80960KB processor and other modules.

The 80960KB Processor and the Local Bus

3

CHAPTER 3
THE 80960KB AND THE LOCAL BUS

The 32-bit multiplexed local bus (L-bus) connects the 80960KB processor to memory and I/O and forms the backbone of any 80960KB processor-based system. This high bandwidth bus provides burst-transfer capability allowing up to four successive 32-bit data word transfers at a maximum rate of one word every clock cycle. In addition to the L-bus signals, the 80960KB processor uses other signals to communicate to other bus masters. This chapter, which describes these signals and the associated operations, follows the outline shown below:

- L-bus states and their relationship to each other
- L-bus signal groups, which consist of address/data and control
- L-bus read, write, and burst transactions
- L-bus timing analysis and timing circuit generation
- Related L-bus operations such as arbitration, interrupt, and reset operations

3.1 OVERVIEW OF THE 80960KB L-BUS

The L-bus forms the data communication path between the various components in a basic 80960KB hardware system. The 80960KB processor utilizes the L-bus to fetch instructions, to manipulate information from both memory and I/O devices, and to respond to interrupts. To perform these functions at a high data rate, the 80960KB processor provides a burst mode, which transfers up to four data words at a maximum rate of one 32-bit word per clock cycle. The 80960KB L-bus includes the following features:

- 32-bit multiplexed address/data path
- High data bandwidth relative to the speed selection of the 80960KB processor
- Four byte enables and a four-word burst capability that allows transfers from 1 to 16 bytes in length
- Support for TTL latches and buffers
- Basic L-Bus States

3.2 BASIC L-BUS STATES

The L-bus has five basic bus states: idle (T_i), address (T_a), data (T_d), recovery (T_r), and wait (T_w). During system operation, the 80960KB processor continuously enters and exits different bus states (see Figure 3-1). The state diagram assumes that only one bus master resides on the L-bus.

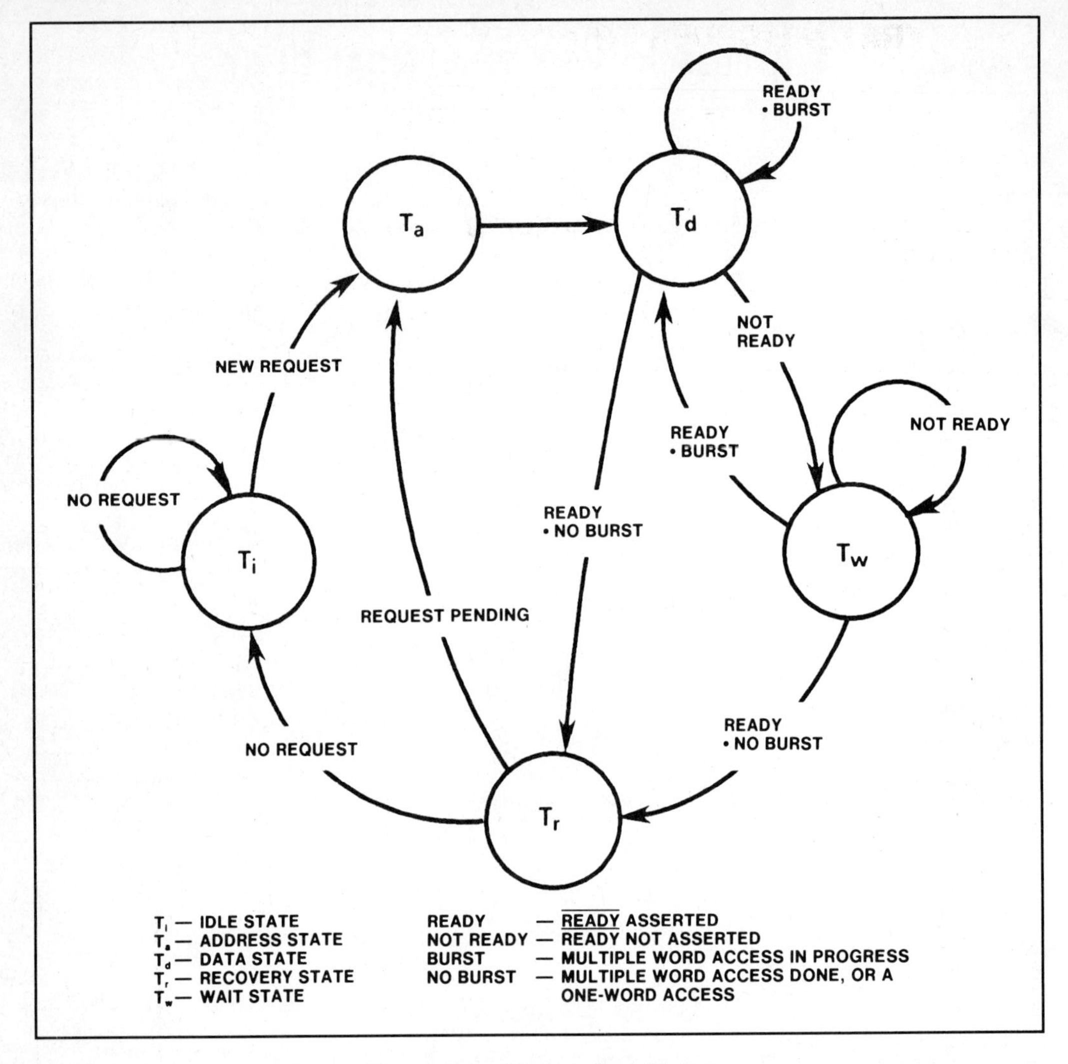

Figure 3-1: Basic L-Bus States

The local bus occupies the idle (T_i) state when no address/data transfers are in progress. When the bus receives a new request, it enters the T_a state to transmit the address.

Following a T_a state, the L-bus enters a T_d state to transmit or receive data on the address/data lines if data is ready. The assertion of the $\overline{\text{READY}}$ signal at the input of the processor indicates the ready state. If the data is not ready, the L-bus enters a T_w state and remains in this state until data is ready. T_w states may repeat as many times as necessary to allow sufficient time for the memory or I/O device to respond.

After a data word transfer in a non-burst transaction, the L-bus exits the T_d or T_w state and enters the recovery (T_r) state. In the case of a burst transaction, the local bus exits the T_d or T_w

state and re-enters the T_d state to transfer the next data word. Once all data words transfer in a burst transaction (up to four), the L-bus enters the T_r state to allow devices on the L-bus to recover.

When the recovery state completes, the L-bus enters the T_i state if no new request is pending. If a request is pending, the L-bus enters the T_a state to transmit the new address.

3.3 L-BUS SIGNAL GROUPS

Signals on the L-bus (see Figure 3-2), consist of two basic groups: address/data, and control. This section provides a description of both groups.

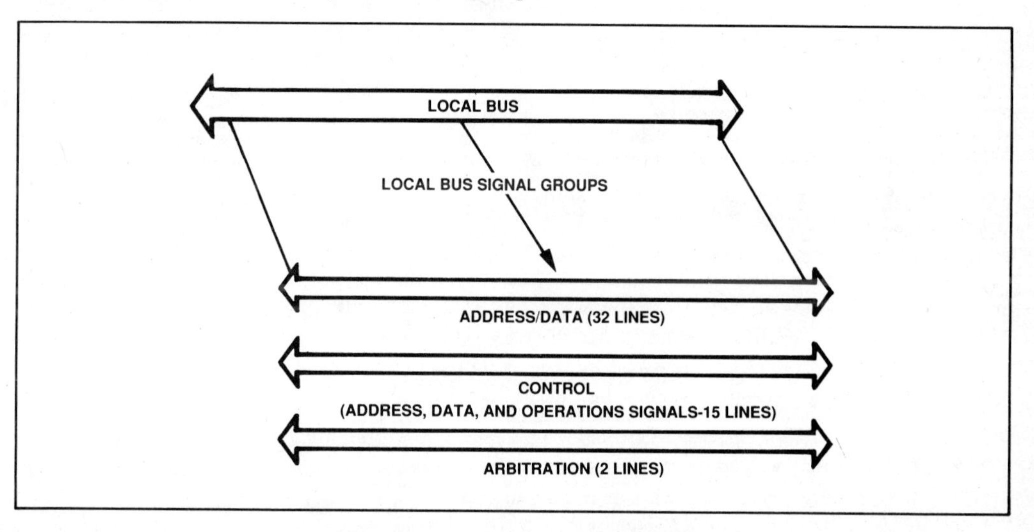

Figure 3-2: L-Bus Signal Groups

3.3.1 Address/Data

The address/data signal group consists of 32 bi-directional lines. These signals multiplex within the processor to serve a dual purpose (depending upon the bus state).

LAD_{31}-LAD_2 — **Local Address/Data$_{31}$** through **Local Address/Data$_2$** represent the address signals on the L-bus during the T_a state. LAD_2 represents the least-significant bit, and LAD_{31} is the most-significant address bit. LAD_{31} through LAD_2 contain a physical word address. The address/data signals float to a high-impedance state when not active.

SIZE (LAD_1-LAD_0) — The **SIZE** signals indicate whether one, two, three, or four words are being transferred during the current transaction. These signals are valid during the T_a state of the L-bus. Refer to Table 1-1 to decode the LAD_1 and LAD_0 signals representing the size of a burst transaction.

Table 3-1: SIZE Signal Decoding

WORD SELECTION	LAD_1	LAD_0
1 word	Low	Low
2 words	Low	High
3 words	High	Low
4 words	High	High

LAD_{31}-LAD_0

Local Address/Data$_{31}$ through **Local Address/Data$_0$** represent the data signals on the L-bus during the T_d and T_w states. LAD_0 is the least-significant bit, and LAD_{31} is the most-significant data bit. The address/data signals float to a high-impedance state when not active.

3.3.2 Control

The control signal group consists of 12 signals that permit the transfer of data. These signals control data buffers, address latches, and other standard interface logic.

$\overline{ALE}$

The **Address Latch Enable** is an active low signal that latches the address from the 80960KB processor. The processor asserts $\overline{ALE}$ during the T_a state and deasserts $\overline{ALE}$ before the beginning of the T_d state. $\overline{ALE}$ floats to a high-impedance level when the processor is not operating on the bus (i.e., the hold state).

$\overline{ADS}$

Address Status is an active low signal that the processor uses to indicate an address state. The processor asserts $\overline{ADS}$ during every T_a state and deasserts it during the next T_d and T_w states. For a burst transaction, the processor asserts $\overline{ADS}$ again every T_d state when $\overline{READY}$ is active in the prior cycle. The $\overline{ADS}$ signal is an open-drain output.

DT/$\overline{R}$

Data Transmit/Receive indicates the direction of data flow to or from the 80960KB processor. For a read operation or an interrupt acknowledge, DT/$\overline{R}$ is low during the T_a, T_d, and T_w states to indicate that data flows into the 80960KB processor. For a write operation, DT/$\overline{R}$ is high during the T_a, T_d, and T_w states to indicate that data flows from the 80960KB processor. DT/$\overline{R}$ never changes states when the processor asserts $\overline{DEN}$. The DT/$\overline{R}$ line is an open-drain output of the 80960KB processor.

$\overline{DEN}$

The **Data Enable** signal (active low) enables data transceivers. The processor asserts $\overline{DEN}$ during all T_d and T_w states The $\overline{DEN}$ line is an open drain-output of the 80960KB-processor.

W/$\overline{R}$

The **Write/Read** signal instructs a memory or I/O device to write or read data on the L-bus. The 80960KB processor asserts W/$\overline{R}$ during a T_a state. The signal remains valid during subsequent T_d and T_w states. W/$\overline{R}$ is an open-drain output of the 80960KB processor.

$\overline{BE_3}$-$\overline{BE_0}$

The **Byte Enable** output signals of the 80960KB processor specify which bytes (up to four) on the 32-bit data bus will transfer during the transaction. Table 1-2 shows the decoding scheme for these signals.

The byte enable signals are valid from the processor before it transfers data, (Figure 1-3) illustrates no wait states . The processor specifies the valid byte enable signals for the first data word during the T_a state. For a four-word burst transaction, the processor asserts the valid byte enable signals for the second word during the first data state (T_{d0}), the third word during the second data state (T_{d1}), and the fourth word during the third data state (T_{d2}). The processor does not define the byte enable signals during the last data state (T_{d3}) for the last word transfer. Although not shown in the diagram, the processor internally latches the byte enable signals of each word, which remain valid during every data or wait state until $\overline{READY}$ is active. At this time, the byte enable signals change during the next T_d state or become undefined for the last data transfer.

The 80960KB processor asserts only adjacent byte enable signals. For example, the processor does not perform a bus operation with only $\overline{BE_0}$ and $\overline{BE_2}$ active. The byte enable lines are open-drain outputs.

Table 3-2: Byte Enable Signal Decoding

Byte Enable Signal	Data Line Selection
$\overline{BE_0}$	LAD_7-LAD_0
$\overline{BE_1}$	LAD_{15}-LAD_8
$\overline{BE_2}$	LAD_{23}-LAD_{16}
$\overline{BE_3}$	LAD_{31}-LAD_{24}

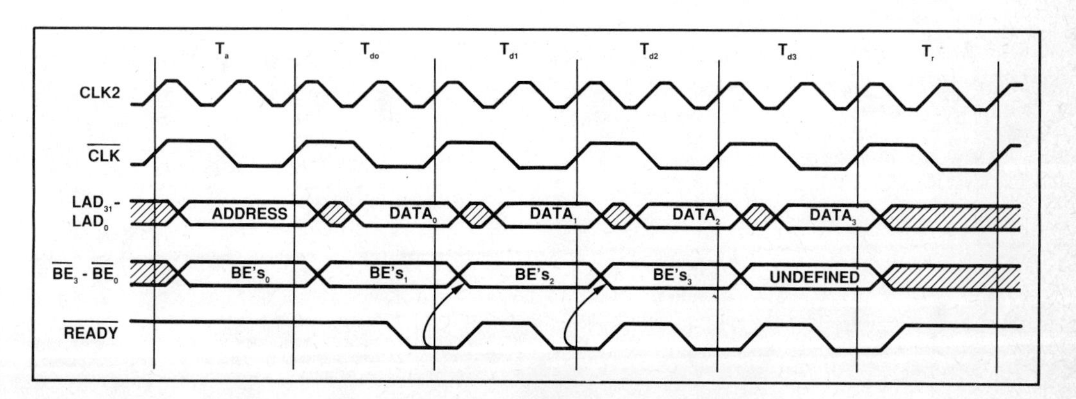

Figure 3-3: Byte Enable Timing Diagram

$\overline{\text{READY}}$

The $\overline{\text{READY}}$ signal indicates that the processor can sample (read) or remove (write) data on the L-bus. If the processor does not see $\overline{\text{READY}}$ asserted following the T_a state or in between T_d states, it generates a T_w state. $\overline{\text{READY}}$ is an active-low input signal to the 80960KB processor.

$\overline{\text{LOCK}}$

Bus $\overline{\text{Lock}}$ prevents other bus masters from gaining control of the L-bus during a bus operation. The processor activates this signal while processing specific operations and instructions.

The 80960KB processor uses the bus $\overline{\text{LOCK}}$ signal when it performs a RMW memory operation. When the processor performs a RMW-Read operation, it asserts the $\overline{\text{LOCK}}$ signal during the T_a state, and asserts and holds $\overline{\text{LOCK}}$ asserted. If the $\overline{\text{LOCK}}$ signal is active, the processor waits until the inactive state before performing the RMW-Read operation. The proccssor deasserts the $\overline{\text{LOCK}}$ signal during the T_a state when it performs a RMW-Write operation.

The 80960KB processor also asserts the $\overline{\text{LOCK}}$ signal during the interrupt acknowledge sequence. $\overline{\text{LOCK}}$ is an input and an open-drain output signal from the 80960KB processor. $\overline{\text{LOCK}}$ must be pulled up if unused.

CACHE

The **CACHE** signal specifies whether or not external logic can cache the current access. The 80960KB processor asserts CACHE during the T_a state. The CACHE signal is undefined during the T_d and T_w states. The CACHE signal floats to a high-impedance state when the L-bus is not acquired.

Table 3-3 summarizes the L-bus signals.

Table 3-3: Summary of L-Bus Signals

SIGNAL GROUP	SIGNAL SYMBOL	SIGNAL FUNCTION	ACTIVE STATE	TYPE OF OUTPUT AND DIRECTION
Local Address/Data	Address (LAD_{31}-LAD_2)	32-bit address	T_a	3-state (O)
Local Address/Data	Data (LAD_{31}-LAD_0)	32-bit data	T_d, T_w	3-state (I/O)
Local Address/Data	Data (LAD_1-LAD_0)	Specifies number of words to transfer	T_a	3-state (O)
Control	$\overline{ALE}$	Enables Address Latch	T_a	3-state (O)
Control	$\overline{ADS}$	Identifies an Address State	T_a, T_d, (Note 1)	Open-drain (O)
Control	$DT/\overline{R}$	Controls direction of data flow	T_a, T_d, T_w	Open-drain (O)
Control	$\overline{DEN}$	Enables data transceiver/latch	T_d, T_w	Open-drain (O)
Control	$W/\overline{R}$	Read/write Command	T_a, T_d, T_w	Open-drain (O)
Control	$\overline{BE_3}$-$\overline{BE_0}$	Specifies which data bytes to transfer	T_a, T_d^2, T_w^2 Note 2	Open-drain (O)
Control	$\overline{READY}$	Indicates data is ready to transfer	Note 3	N/A (I)
Control	$\overline{LOCK}$	Locks bus	any	Open-drain (I/O)
Control	CACHE	Indicates cacheable transaction	T_a	3-state (O)

Note: 1 except first T_d
2 except last T_d, T_w
3 sampled during T_d and T_w

The 80960KB processor uses additional pins to control the execution of instructions and to interface to other bus masters. These pins include the arbitration, interrupt, error, and reset signals. Each of these signal groups are explained in following sections.

3.4 L-BUS TRANSACTIONS

The 80960KB processor uses the L-bus signals to perform transactions to transfer data to (or from) the CPU from (or to) another component. During a transaction, the 80960KB processor can transfer up to four words of data for a single address to enhance system throughput. This is especially useful when loading cache memory.

3.4.1 Clock Signal

The 80960KB hardware system typically uses two clock signals (CLK2 and CLK) to synchronize the transitions between L-bus states. CLK2 provides the clock input to the 80960KB. This clock is also the system clock. Additional logic develops the optional CLK clock signal, which defines the state transition boundaries at one-half the frequency of CLK2. The CLK signal provides a convenient indicator of L-bus boundaries and can drive peripheral devices. CLK is neither an input nor an output of the processor. Figure 3-4 illustrates the relationship between the system CLK2 and CLK.

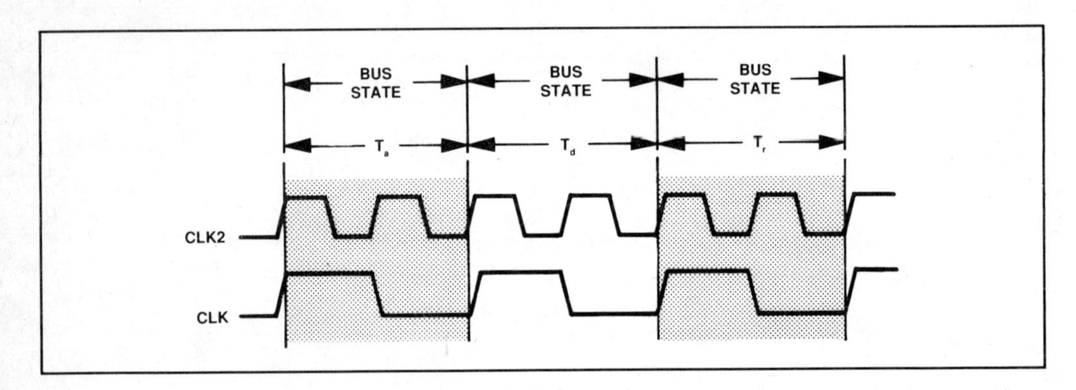

Figure 3-4: Clock Relationships

3.4.2 Basic Read

A basic transaction reads or writes one data word. Figure 3-5 shows a typical timing diagram for a read transaction. See the 80960KB processor data sheet for exact timing relationships. The following sequence of events explains the flow of the timing diagram. For simplicity, the figure shows no wait states.

1. The 80960KB processor generates several signals during the T_a state.
   - It transmits the address on the address/data lines. LAD_1 and LAD_0 specify a single word transaction.
   - It asserts $\overline{ALE}$ to latch the address.
   - It asserts $\overline{ADS}$.
   - It asserts $\overline{BE_3}$-$\overline{BE_0}$ to specify which bytes the processor uses when reading the data word.
   - It brings W/$\overline{R}$ low to denote a read operation.
   - It brings DT/$\overline{R}$ low to define the input direction of the data transceivers.
2. During the T_d state, several actions occur.
   - The 80960KB processor asserts $\overline{DEN}$ to enable data transceivers.

- External timing asserts $\overline{READY}$ logic allowing the processor to receive data from the storage devices. If $\overline{READY}$ is not asserted, L-bus enters a T_w state. The T_w state repeats until the system asserts $\overline{READY}$.

3. The T_r state follows the data state. This allows the system components adequate time (one processor clock cycle) to remove their outputs from the bus before the 80960KB processor generates the next address on the address/data lines. During the T_r state, W/$\overline{R}$, DT/$\overline{R}$, and $\overline{DEN}$ are inactive.

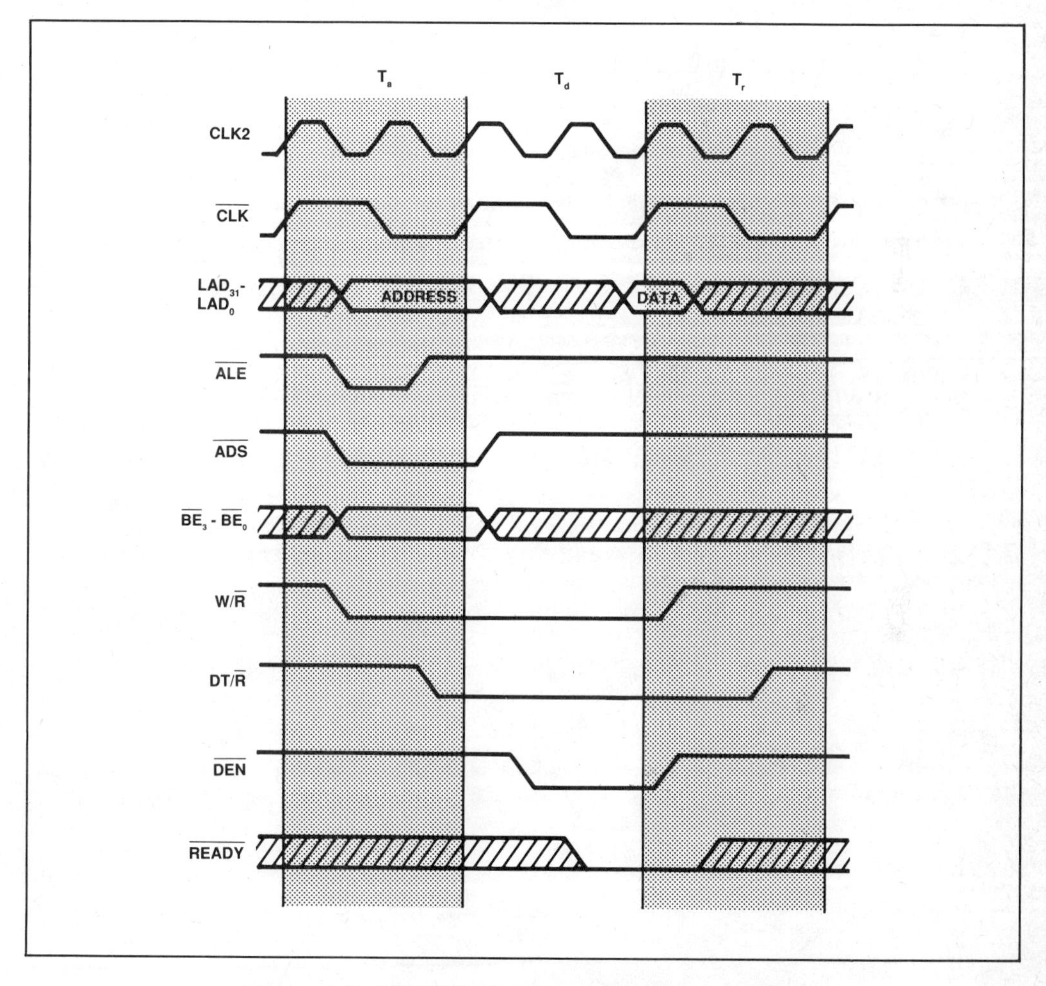

Figure 3-5: 80960KB Processor Read Transaction

3.4.3 Write Transaction

Figure 3-6 shows a typical diagram for a write transaction using one wait state. The following sequence of events explains the flow of the timing diagram.

1. Similar to the read transaction, the 80960KB processor generates several signals during the T_a state.
   - It transmits the address on the address/data lines. LAD_1 and LAD_0 specify a single word transaction.
   - It asserts $\overline{ALE}$ to latch the address.
   - It asserts $\overline{ADS}$.
   - It asserts $\overline{BE}_3$-$\overline{BE}_0$ to specify which bytes the processor uses when writing the data word.
   - It brings W/$\overline{R}$ high to denote a write operation.
   - It brings DT/$\overline{R}$ high to define the direction input for the data transceivers.
2. During the T_d state, several actions occur.
   - The 80960KB places the data on the address/data lines.
   - The 80960KB processor asserts $\overline{DEN}$ to enable data transceivers.
   - External timing does *not* assert $\overline{READY}$. Consequently, the processor holds data on the LAD lines.
3. During the T_w state, the processor asserts $\overline{READY}$ and writes data to the storage device. Note that W/$\overline{R}$, DT/$\overline{R}$, and $\overline{DEN}$ remain constant until the bus state after the assertion of the signal $\overline{READY}$.
4. The T_r state follows the wait state. During the T_r state, W/$\overline{R}$, DT/$\overline{R}$, and $\overline{DEN}$ are inactive.

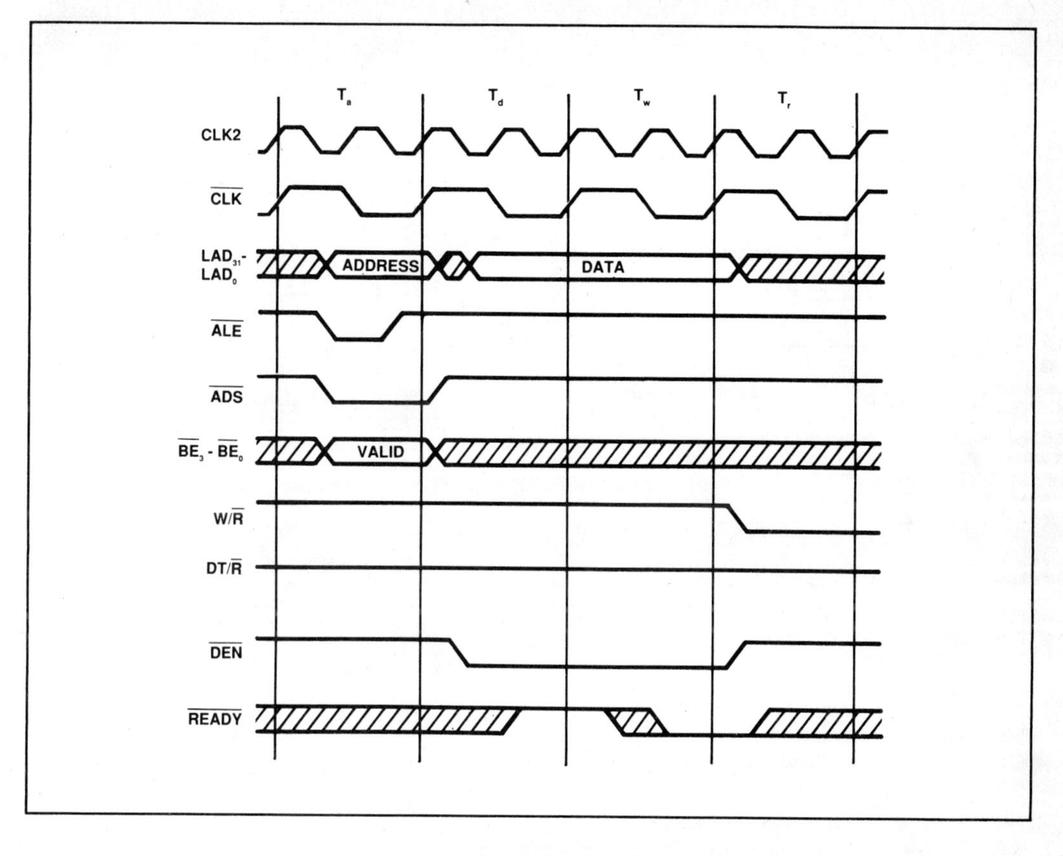

Figure 3-6: 80960KB Processor Write Transaction

3.4.4 Burst Transactions

The 80960KB processor supports burst transactions that read or write up to four words (16 contiguous bytes) at a maximum rate of one word every L-bus cycle. If a transaction crosses a 16-byte boundary, the 80960KB processor automatically splits the transaction into two accesses.

Figure 3-7 illustrates the process. The top half of the figure shows the initial location of 12 bytes of data contained in registers G4 through G6. If the task of the instruction is to move this data to an address beginning at address A_{16} in memory, the ending results would place memory as shown (also in the top half of the figure). Notice that a new 16-byte boundary begins at address 10_{16}. Since the processor stores 6 of the 12 bytes of data after this 16-byte boundary occurs, the processor needs to split the transaction into two 2-word bursts.

In burst one, (bottom half of Figure 3-7), the processor loads the first word (contents 5678_{16}) at address A_{16} and B_{16}. The contents of address 8_{16} and 9_{16} remain unchanged. The processor then loads the second word of burst one (contents $FACE_{16}$ and 1234_{16}) at addresses C_{16} through F_{16}. At this point, the processor performs another burst cycle and transfers the remaining data in address locations 10_{16} through 15_{16} using the same process described above.

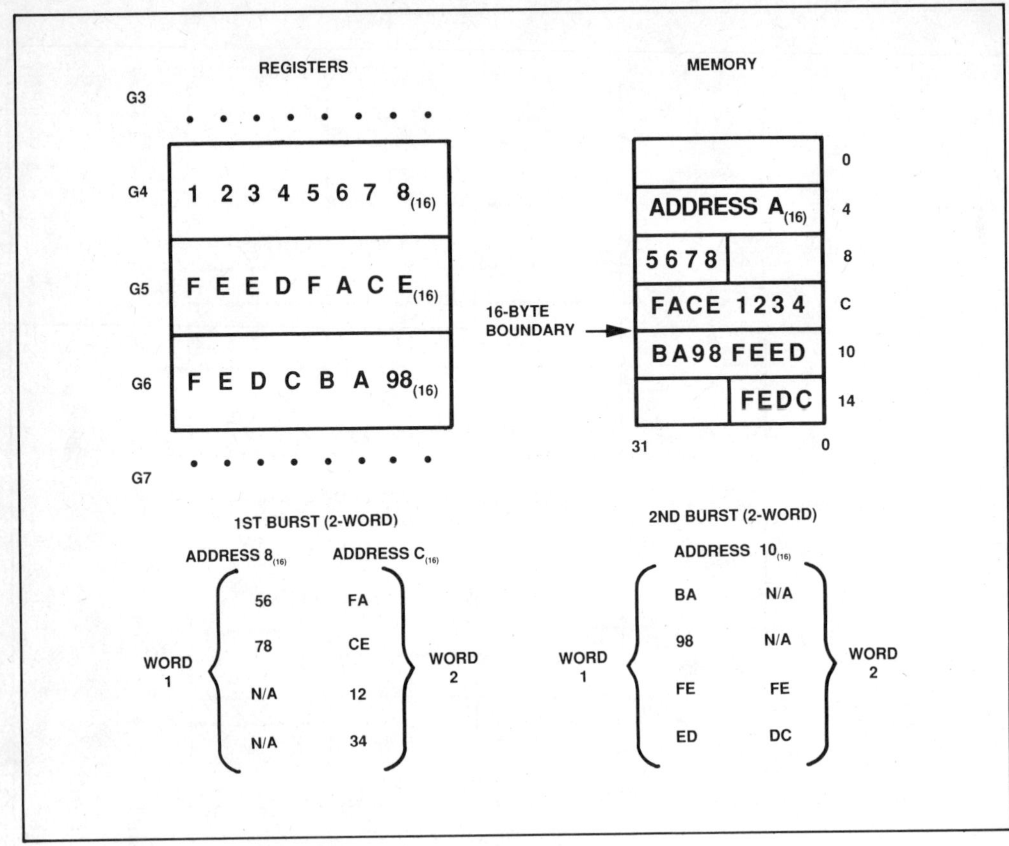

Figure 3-7: Processor 2-word Burst Transaction

The byte enable signals are valid for each word. This allows partial word write operations to contiguous bytes within a word. The CACHE output signal during a T_a state applies to all words of a burst transaction.

A burst read or write transaction is similar to a single-word read or write operation. It differs primarily in the number of data words that the processor transfers; a basic transaction always transfers one word, while a burst transaction transfers up to four data words. For a burst transaction, the byte enable signals operate during the T_a state and subsequently during every T_d or T_w state before the data word transfers. Figure 3-8 shows the timing for a three-word burst read transaction without wait states.

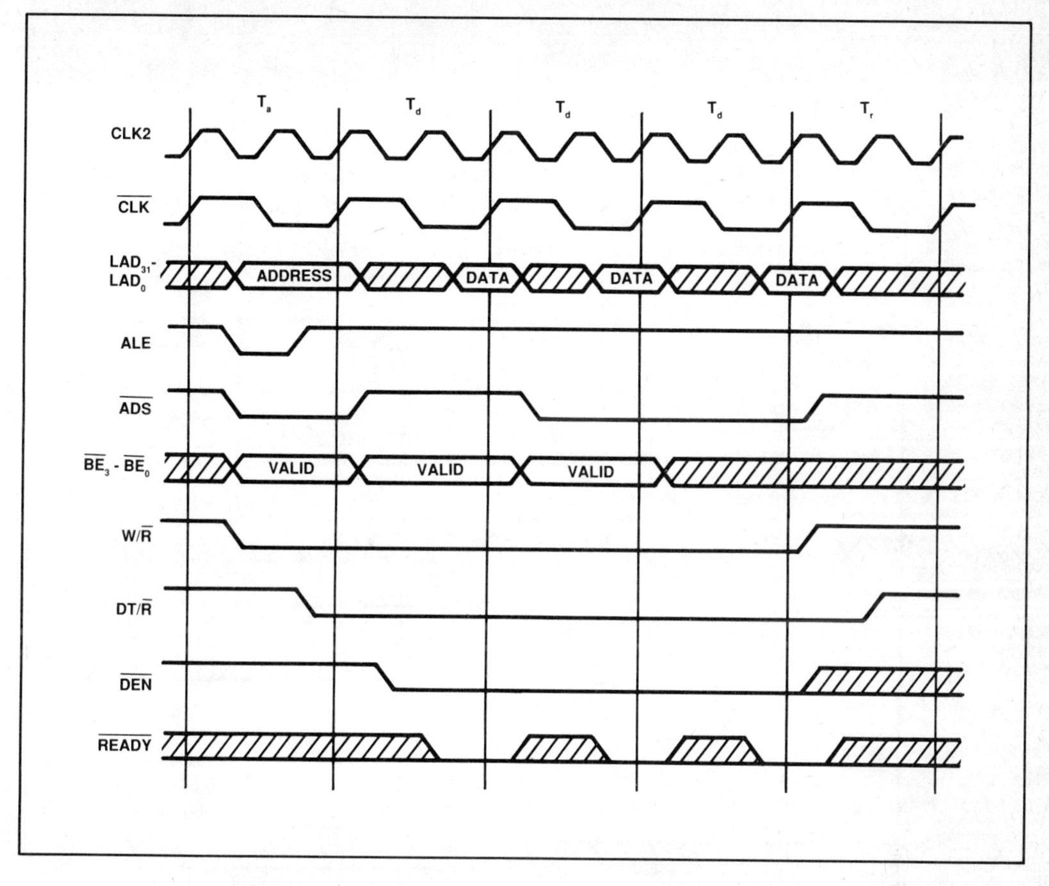

Figure 3-8: Processor 3-word Burst Read Transaction

Figure 3-9 shows the timing for a two-word burst write transaction with a wait state occurring during transfer of the first word. Note that the byte enable signals remain constant until the data state following the time when the system asserts $\overline{\text{READY}}$.

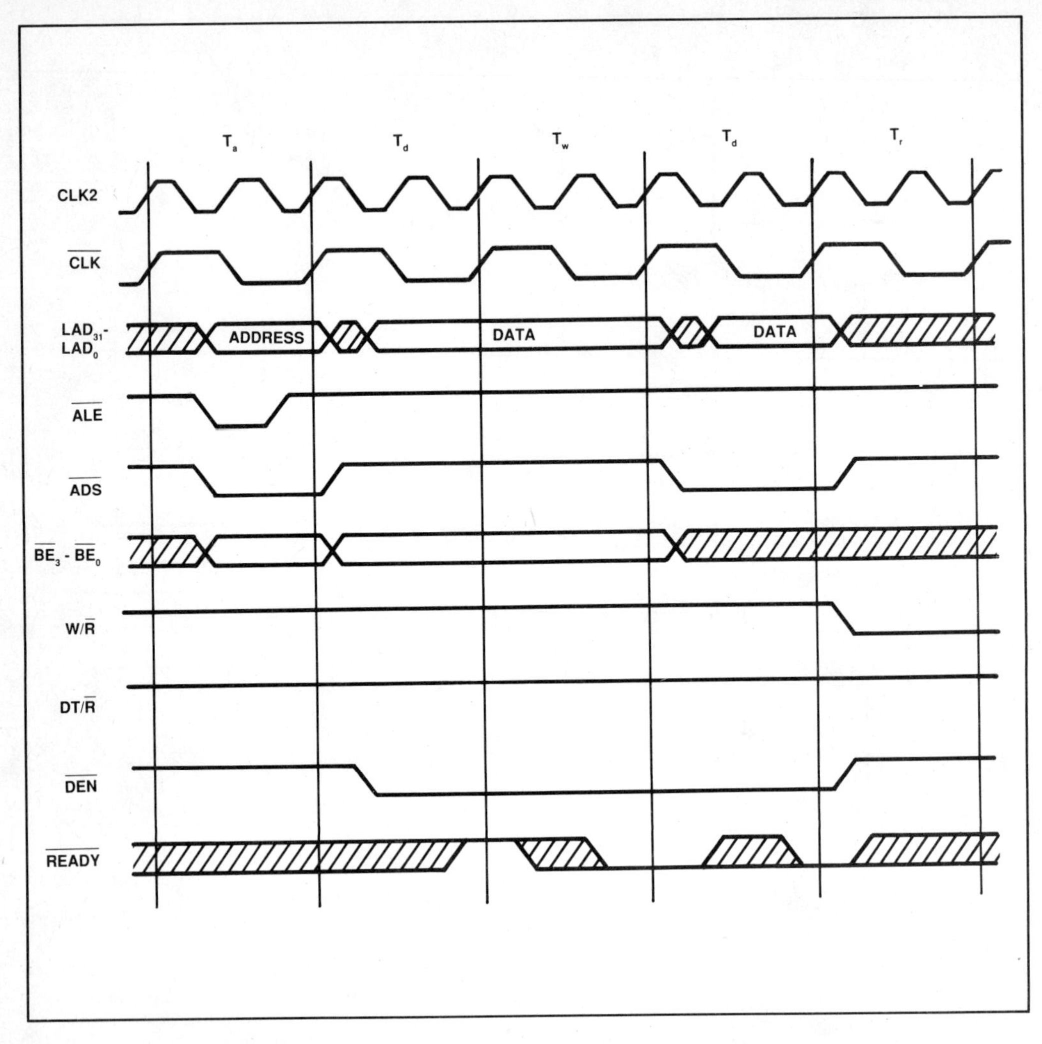

Figure 3-9: Processor 2-word Burst Write Transaction

3.5 TIMING GENERATION

In an 80960KB processor-based system, the design must provide circuitry that generates timing signals for the clock and reset inputs. To generate these signals, the logic should minimize skew and produce quick rise and fall times. This section describes a typical circuit that synthesizes the clock signal. The *Reset and Initialization* section of this chapter discusses the RESET timing generation.

3.5.1 80960KB Processor Clock Requirements

In order to design a clock generator, you must first examine the clock input specifications. The following four parameters specify the clock pulse.

1. The clock fall time (t_f)
2. The clock low time (t_l)
3. The clock rise time (t_r)
4. The clock period (t_{cyc})

The time required to go from 90% of the difference between the high and low voltage levels (to 10% of the difference) or from low to high is defined as the clock fall (rise) time. The clock low time specifies the time required for the clock to remain within 10% of the low voltage level. Similarly, the clock high time specifies the required time for the clock pulse to remain within 10% of the high voltage level. The clock period is the sum of $t_f + t_l + t_r + t_h$.

The clock generator must have fast enough rise and fall times to comply with the requirements for high and low time and the overall clock period. For example, consider a clock pulse with a 50% duty cycle at 50 MHz. The clock period specifies a minimum of 25 ns, a low time at a minimum of 8 ns, and high time at a minimum of 8 ns. This implies that the sum of the rise and fall time must not be greater than 9 ns. Thus, the clock design should have rise and fall times not greater than 4.5 ns each. Besides specifying a maximum clock rate, the 80960KB processor requires a minimum CLK2 rate of 8 MHz to maintain the state of the internal dynamic cells. Due to this minimum frequency requirement, you can not disable the clock to single-step the 80960KB processor.

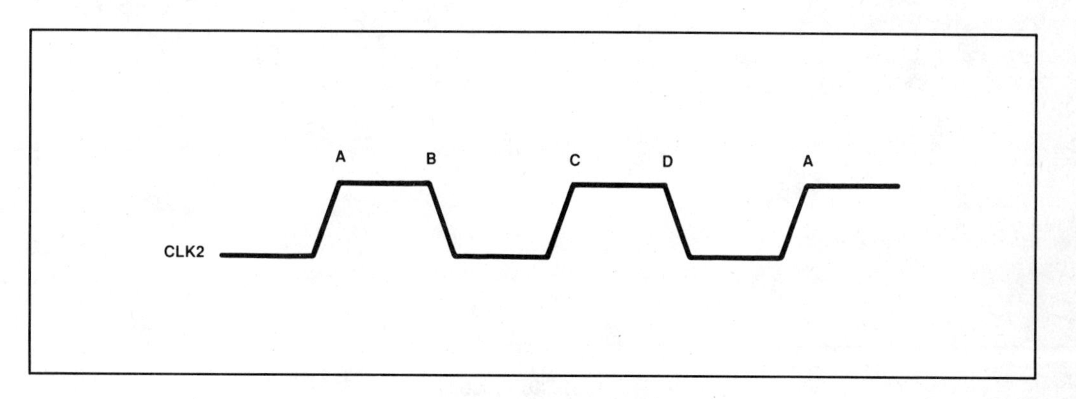

Figure 3-10: CLK2 Edges

3.5.2 Clock Generation

The clock input to the 80960KB is twice the part frequency, i.e., 50 MHz for a 25 MHz 80960KB (the 25 MHz number refers to the bus frequency). Bus cycle boundaries and processor operations occur at one-half the input clock frequency. However, the processor uses all input clock edges. Referring to Figure 3-10, first rising edge of the input clock, or

CLK2, is called the *A* edge. The subsequent three edges are called *B*, *C*, and *D*. *A* clock edges occur at one half of the CLK2 frequency. Most of the outputs from the processor assert on an *A* edge and all inputs are sampled on an *A* edge.

Figure 3-11 shows a typical clock circuit that provides a low skew CLK2 source. The circuitry also generates phase 1 (PH1) and inverted CLK2. PH1 marks the edges of CLK2 and overlaps the inverted CLK2's *B* and *C* edges. The inverted CLK2 is a clock with rising *B* and *D* edges to generate memory write strobes.

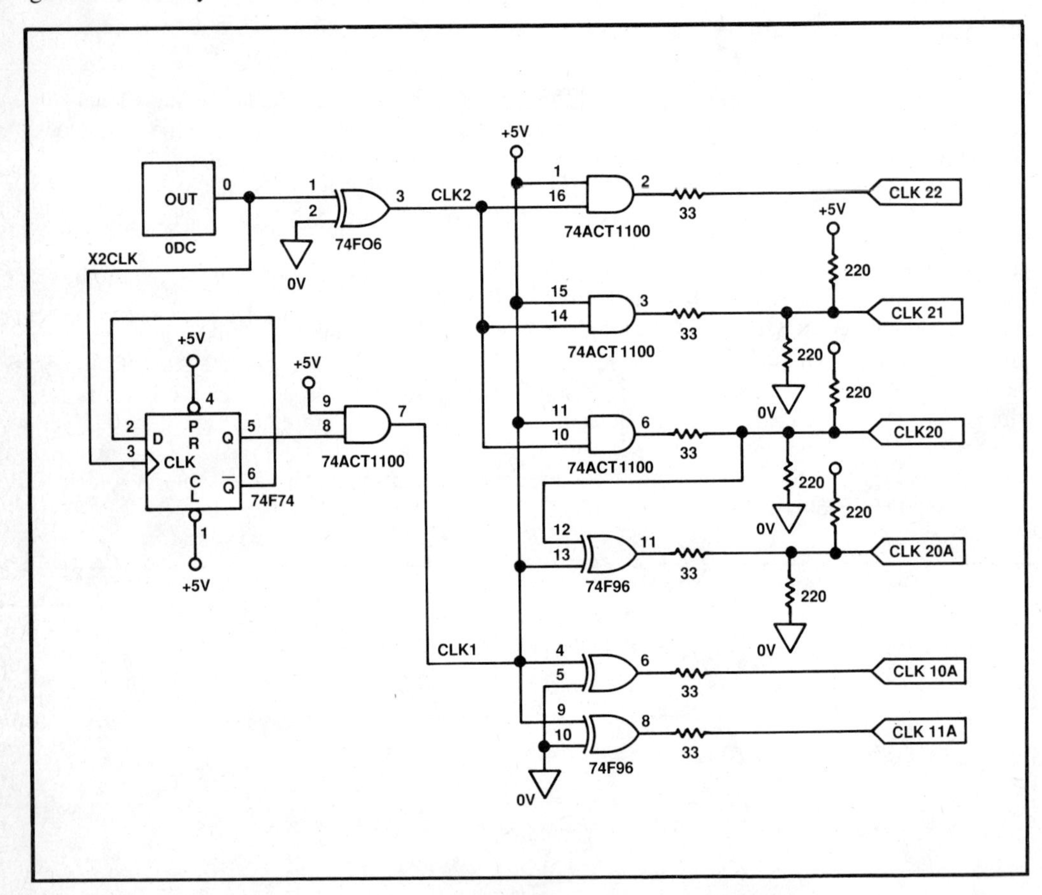

Figure 3-11: Typical Clock Logic for 80960KB

The CLK2 source is an oscillator whose output feeds into a XOR gate and a D-flip-flop. The XOR gate ensures that the inverted CLK2 and PH1 signals skew only from the rise time of the flip-flop. An AND gate drives the CLK2 signals. The gates provide a fast rise time and high current drive, which allows designs to use termination resistors. This AND package generates three CLK2 signals CLK20, CLK21, and CLK22 to minimize loading and trace lengths.

All clock nets should be terminated to reduce reflections. The clock logic example provides both series and parallel termination. Series termination places a small resistance next to the clock driver which has the effect of slowing the signal rise times thus reducing high-frequency

reflections. Parallel termination places a resistance roughly equal to the characteristic impedance of the board traces at the end of the clock trace. This eliminates the 100% reflections that normally occur at the end of a trace. The design needs only one of these termination types (figure 3-11 shows both).

Two additional clock signals shown in the circuit above are PH10 and PH11 which provide phase information to bus control logic.

These clock signals exhibit a slight skew with respect to CLK2. The CLK2 circuitry clocks the gates that use PH10 and PH11. These signals must therefore meet the setup and hold time specifications with respect to CLK2.

3.5.3 Open-Drain Pullups

Several of the 80960KB outputs use high-current open-drain drivers allowing the signals to be wire-ORed in systems with more than one bus master. The data sheet specifies the maximum fall time of these signals as 30 nS for a 20 MHz part. The rise time, however, is a function of both the maximum float delay specification of 5 to 20 nS and the pullup resistor values. If you want the signal rise time to equal the fall time, then the pullup resistor must be able to charge the load capacitance within 10 nS after the driver turns off. The equation for the voltage on a capacitor charging from voltage V_f through a resistor as a function of time is:

1. $V(t) = V_f(1 - e^{-t/RC})$

   solving for R:

2. $R = -t/(C(\ln((V_f - V)/V_f))$

   For an open-drain driver connected to a node at 0 V, assuming a worst case power supply voltage of 4.5V, the V_f available to charge the load capacitance will 4.5 V. Assuming a 50 pF load capacitance and assuming V equals 2.0 V (TTL high level) then:

3. $R = -10nS/(50pF(\ln(4.5V - 2.0V)/4.5V)) = 340$ Ohms

If we recalculate the above formulas assuming that the node is at 0.45 V (data sheet voltage specification at 25 mA) then V_f becomes (4.5V - 0.45V) and V becomes (2.0V - 0.45V) giving an R of 415 Ohms. Since the driver *sinks* only 13 mA with a 415 Ohm pullup and 5.5 V of supply voltage the VOL will be less than 0.45V. Thus, the lower 340 Ohm value represents the worst case. If we assume a 100 pF load capacitance and wish to maintain the 30 nS (float delay + 10 nS) rise time then the design requires a pull-up resistor of approximately 340/2 or 170 Ohms.

3.6 ARBITRATION

When multiple bus masters exist, an arbitration process exchanges control of the bus. The process assumes two bus masters: a default bus master that controls the bus, and another that requests control of the bus when it performs an operation (e.g., a DMA controller). More than two bus masters may exist on the L-bus, but this requires external arbitration logic. However, since one 80960KB processor alone uses over one-half of the bandwidth, no more than two 80960KB processors may reside on an L-bus.

This section examines bus arbitration, bus states, and presents timing diagrams for differing combinations of two bus masters (see Table 3-4).

Table 3-4: Combination of Bus Masters

Bus Master that Controls the bus by Default	Bus Master that Requests Control of the Bus
(CASE 1) 80960KB PROCESSOR	I/O DEVICE
(CASE 2) 80960KB PROCESSOR	80960KB PROCESSOR
(CASE 3) I/O DEVICE	80960KB PROCESSOR

3.6.1 Single 80960KB Processor on the L-Bus

For the first case, the 80960KB processor controls the L-bus, and a master I/O peripheral (such as a DMA controller) requests control of the bus. The 80960KB processor and the I/O peripheral device exchange control of the bus with two signals: the hold request (HOLD) and hold acknowledge (HLDA) signals.

HOLD is an input signal of the 80960KB processor, which indicates that the master I/O peripheral requests control of the L-bus. When the peripheral asserts HOLD, the 80960KB processor surrenders control of the bus after it completes the current bus transaction. The 80960KB processor then acknowledges transfer of L-bus control to the requesting bus master when it asserts HLDA.

3.6.2 State Diagram

Figure 1-12 shows the state diagram for an L-bus with two bus masters: an 80960KB processor, and an I/O peripheral device. This state diagram includes a hold state (T_h) in addition to the five basic states described in the *Basic L-Bus States* section of this chapter. The 80960KB processor enters the T_h state when it surrenders control of the bus. It can enter the T_h state from the T_i, T_r, T_d, or T_w state. When the 80960KB processor regains control of the L-bus, it enters the T_a state if a new request is pending, or it enters the T_i state if no new request is pending.

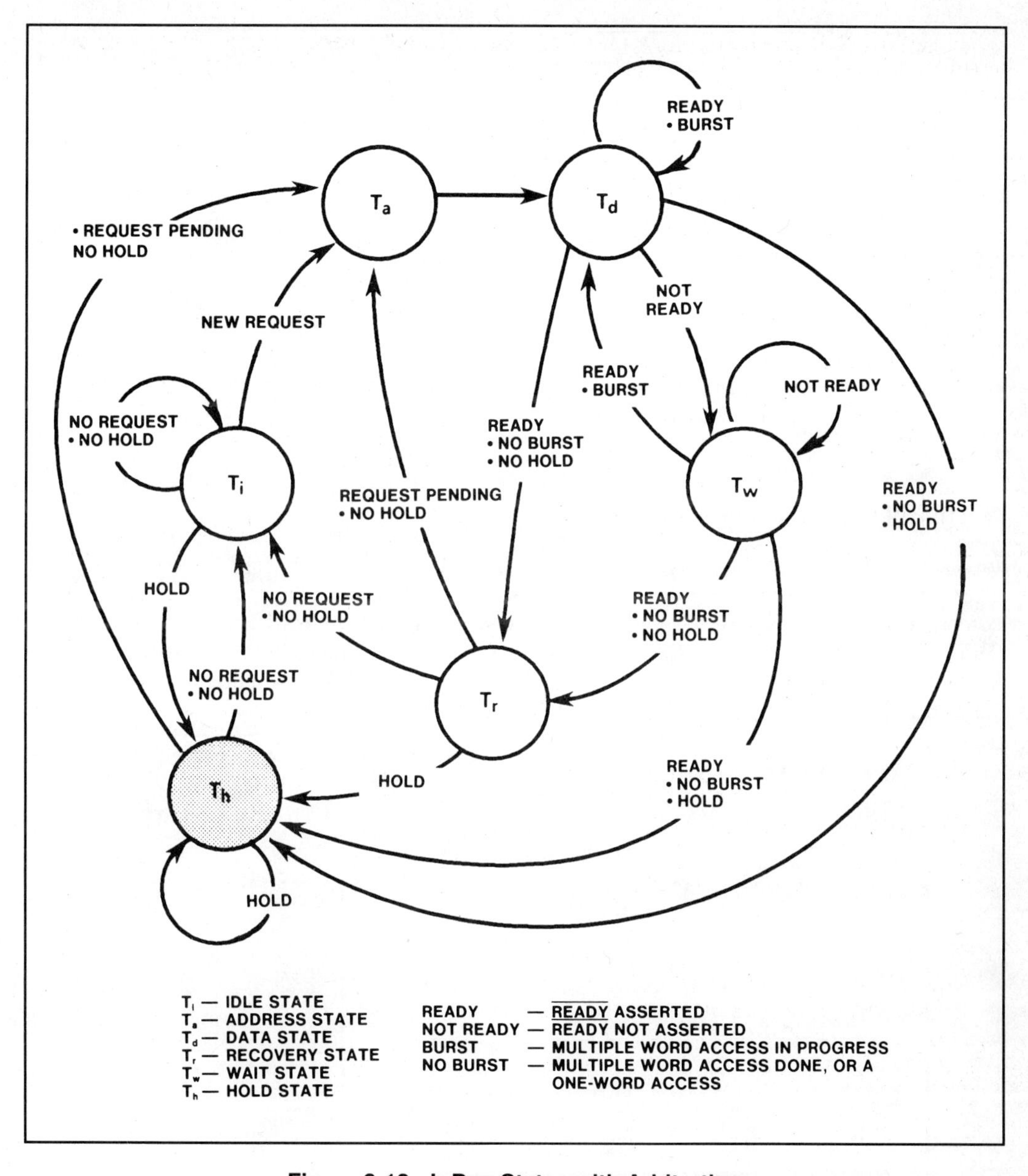

Figure 3-12: L-Bus States with Arbitration

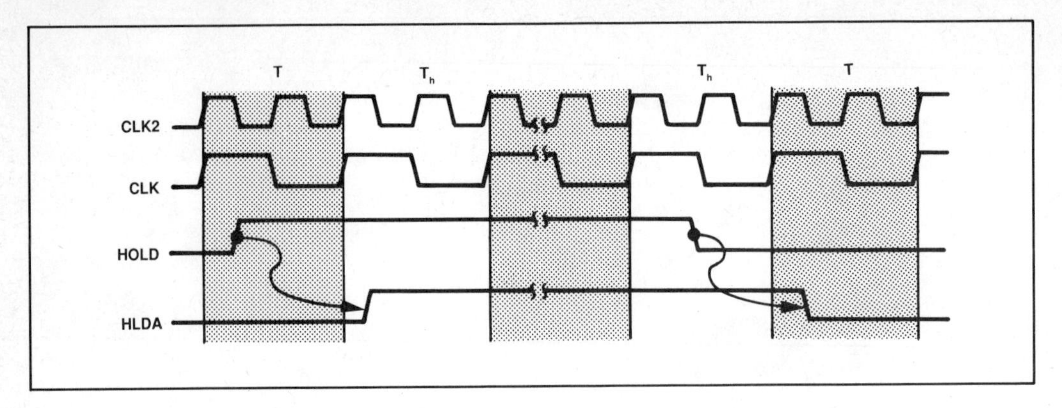

Figure 3-13: Arbitration Timing Diagram for a Bus Master

3.6.3 Arbitration Timing

Figure 3-13 illustrates the arbitration timing diagram. The initial *T* state represents the last cycle of a transaction in which the processor asserts a READY signal or a t_i state. The 80960KB processor receives a request to relinquish control of the bus when the device asserts HOLD. After the 80960KB processor completes the current transaction, it responds to this request when it floats the tri-state output signals and deasserts the open-drain output signals. The HLDA output signal, however, remains active as the 80960KB processor enters a T_h state. During the T_h state, the CPU ignores all input signals except HOLD and RESET. When the device deasserts the HOLD input, the 80960KB processor exits the T_h state, deasserts HLDA, and enters a T_a state (for pending request) or it enters the T_i state (if no request is pending).

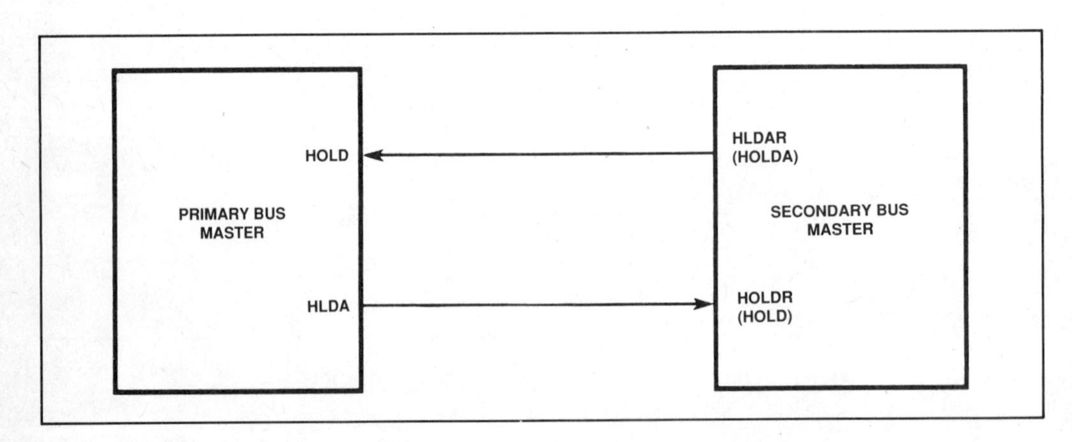

Figure 3-14: Arbitration Connection between Two 80960KB Processors

3.6.4 Two 80960KB Processors on the L-Bus

For the next case, two 80960KB processors reside on the L-bus. During initialization, the design designates Local Processor Number Zero (LPN0) as the Primary Bus Master (PBM), and Local Processor Number One (LPN1) as the Secondary Bus Master (SBM). The exchange process guarantees that neither device is kept off the bus indefinitely. The 80960KB processors use two pins for bus arbitration: the HOLD input pin, and the HLDA output pin. However, the interpretation of these input and output pins differ for the Secondary Bus Master. When the SBM initializes, the pin for the HOLD input signal represents the Hold Acknowledge Received (HLDAR) input signal. The assertion of HLDAR indicates that the PBM relinquishes control of the L-bus. Similarly, the HLDA output signal of the SBM represents the hold request (HOLDR) output signal. The SBM asserts HOLDR to request acquisition of the L-bus. In this manner, you can accomplish bus arbitration between two 80960KB processors; connect HOLD of the PBM to HOLDR of the SBM, and connect HLDA of the PBM to the HLDAR of the SBM (see Figure 3-14).

3.6.5 Bus states for Two 80960KB Processors

The state diagram for the SBM is shown in Figure 3-15. Because of two 80960KB processors, the state diagram includes the $\overline{LOCK}$ signal. The SBM requests control of the L-bus when it asserts HOLDR and subsequently enters the hold request (T_{hr}) state provided that the bus is not locked (locked means that the PBM is currently executing a Read-Modify-Write operation and is asserting the $\overline{LOCK}$ signal and the SBM has a pending operation that would assert $\overline{LOCK}$.). The SBM remains in the T_{hr} state until it acquires control of the L-bus. The SBM acquires control when it receives HLDAR. The SBM returns to the T_i state and deasserts HOLDR if the PBM asserts LOCK to execute a Read-Modify-Write operation and the SBM has a pending operation that would assert $\overline{LOCK}$.

The SBM gains control of the bus when it asserts HLDAR, but only if the PBM is not holding the bus. After gaining control of the L-bus, the SBM performs the requested transaction and, if necessary, enters a T_w state. At the end of a transaction, the SBM enters the T_r state and deasserts HOLDR for at least one processor clock cycle to allow another peripheral bus master to gain access (if necessary). If another request is pending, the SBM enters the T_{hr} state and asserts HOLDR (providing the PBM is not locking the bus). If no request is pending, the SBM returns to the T_i state. The PBM never forces the SBM off the bus.

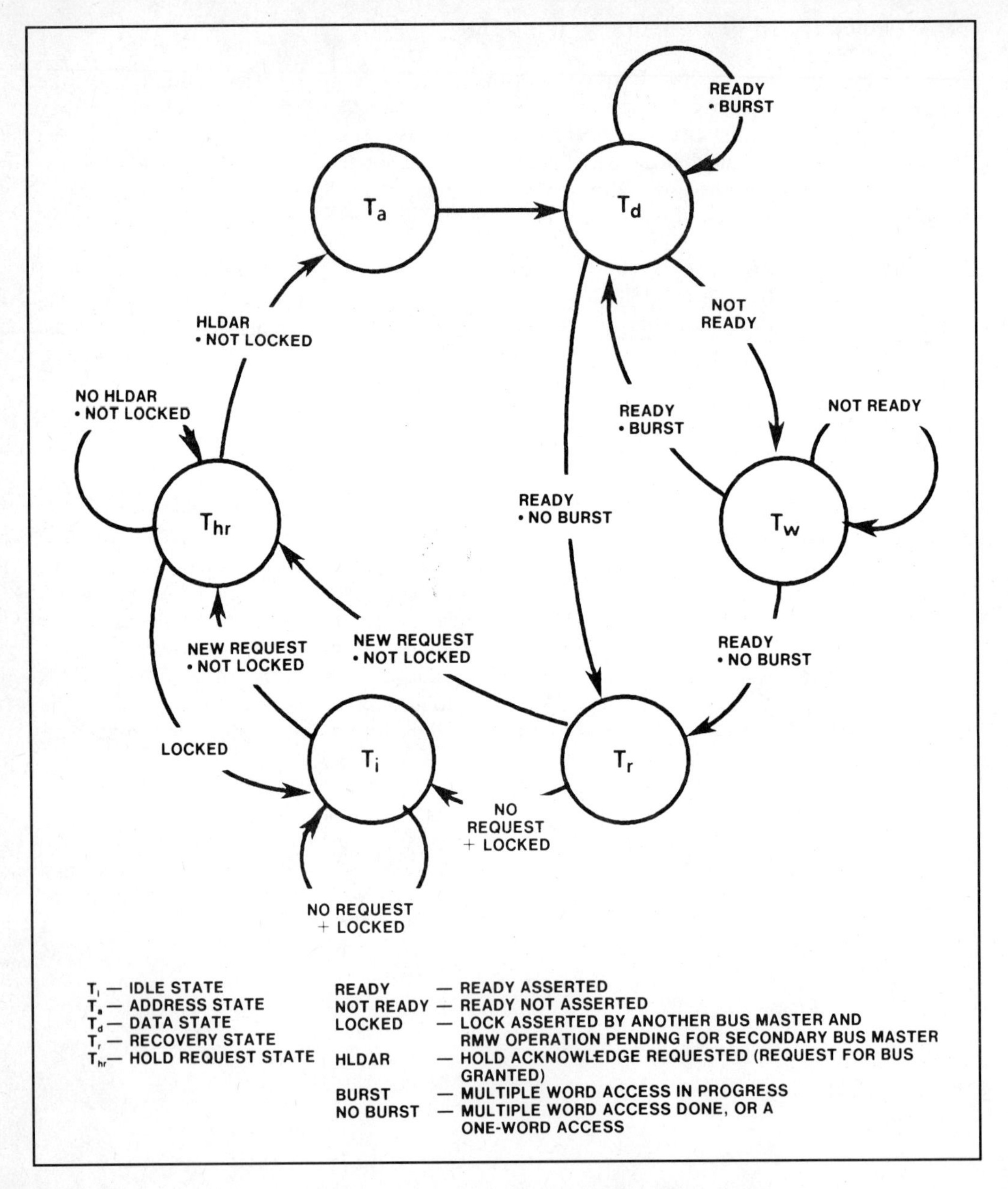

Figure 3-15: L-Bus States for Secondary Bus Master

3.6.6 Arbitration Timing for Two 80960KB Processors

Figure 3-16: shows the timing diagram that the SBM follows when it acquires and relinquishes the L-bus. The SBM enters into the Hold/Request (T_{hr}) state and asserts the HOLDR signal. It remains in the T_{hr} state until the PBM asserts HLDAR, indicating that the SBM has gained control of the L-bus. At the end of the transaction, the SBM enters the T_r state and deasserts HOLDR. Except for HOLDR, the output signals of the SBM enter the high-impedance state. In the case where the output signals are open-drain outputs, the SBM will deassert them.

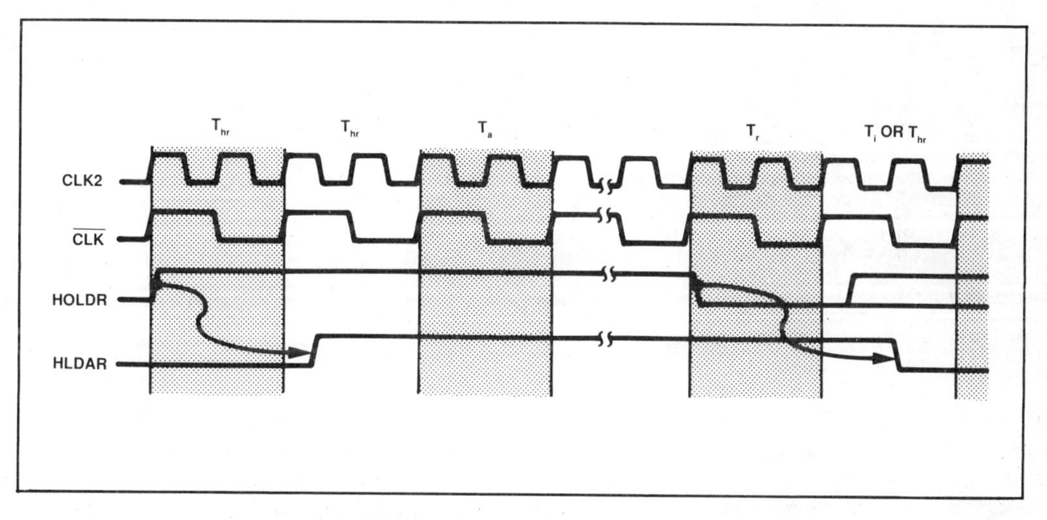

Figure 3-16: Arbitration Timing Diagram for an SBM

3.6.7 Bus Exchange Example Between Two 80960KB Processors

Figure 3-17 shows an example of bus arbitration between a PBM and a SBM using the arbitration signals. Each bus master performs a one-word read and a two-word write transaction to demonstrate the fastest possible bus exchanges.

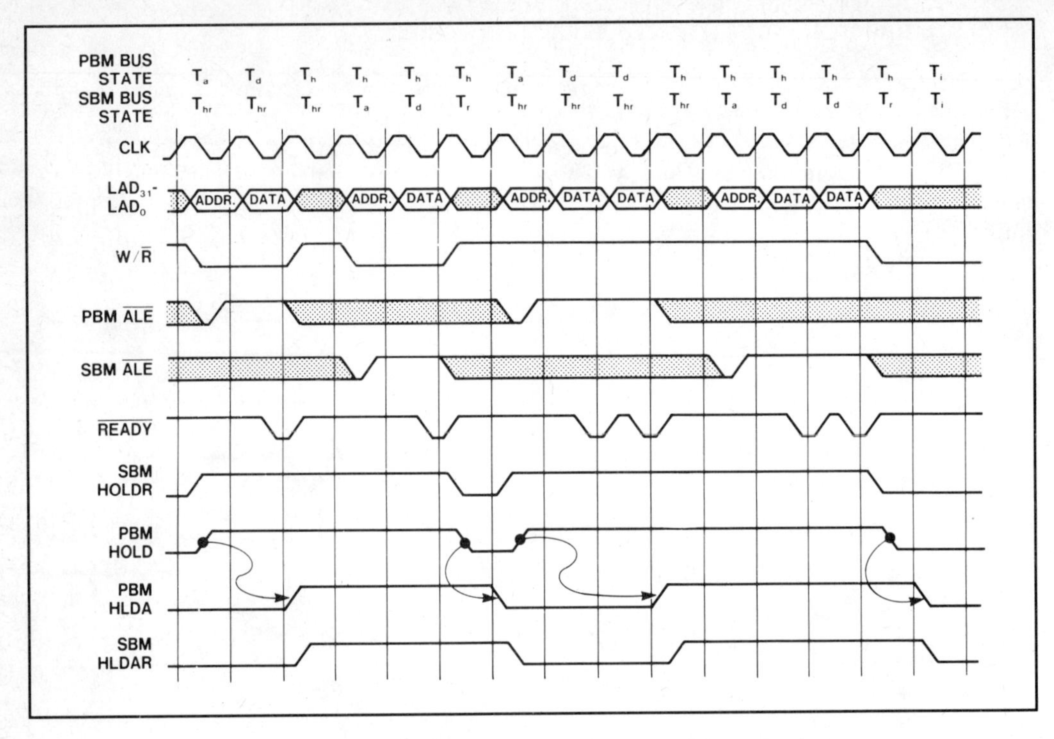

Figure 3-17: Example of a Bus Exchange Transaction

While the PBM performs a read transaction, the SBM requests control of the L-bus when it asserts HOLDR and enters the T_{hr} state. It remains in this state until the PBM grants the request when it asserts HLDA following the completion of the read transaction. After granting the request, the PBM enters the T_h state and remains in this state until it deasserts its HOLD signal. When the SBM completes the read transaction, it deasserts HOLDR and returns control to the PBM.

The PBM now performs a two-word write transaction after it deasserts HLDA. The SBM again requests control when it asserts the HOLDR signal and enters the T_{hr} state. When the PBM completes the two-word write transaction, it grants the request when it asserts HLDA and enters the T_h state. The SBM receives the signal on the HLDAR input and performs a two-word write transaction. When the SBM completes the transaction, it transfers control of the L-bus to the PBM, and both the PBM and the SBM enter the T_i state.

3.6.8 A Peripheral Device As the Default Bus Master

The following text describes another example where a peripheral device controls the L-bus, and the 80960KB processor requests control of the bus to perform operations.

NOTE

This alternative is not advisable because it may hinder system performance.

The exchange process is identical to the one described in the previous section. The 80960KB processor is a SBM and uses two pins for bus arbitration: the HOLDR input pin, and the HLDAR output pin. The state diagram is similar to Figure 3-15. The design, however, does not use the lock conditions for this case.

The peripheral device grants control of the L-bus when it asserts HLDAR following an SBM request of the L-bus. The peripheral device can obtain control of the L-bus again with the deassertion of HLDAR. If this occurs, the 80960KB processor surrenders control of the bus after it completes the current transaction (see Figure 3-18). At that time, the 80960KB processor deasserts the HOLDR signal and places the other output signals into a high-impedance state (or a deasserted open-drain level). The 80960KB processor may again request access to the L-bus when it asserts HOLDR.

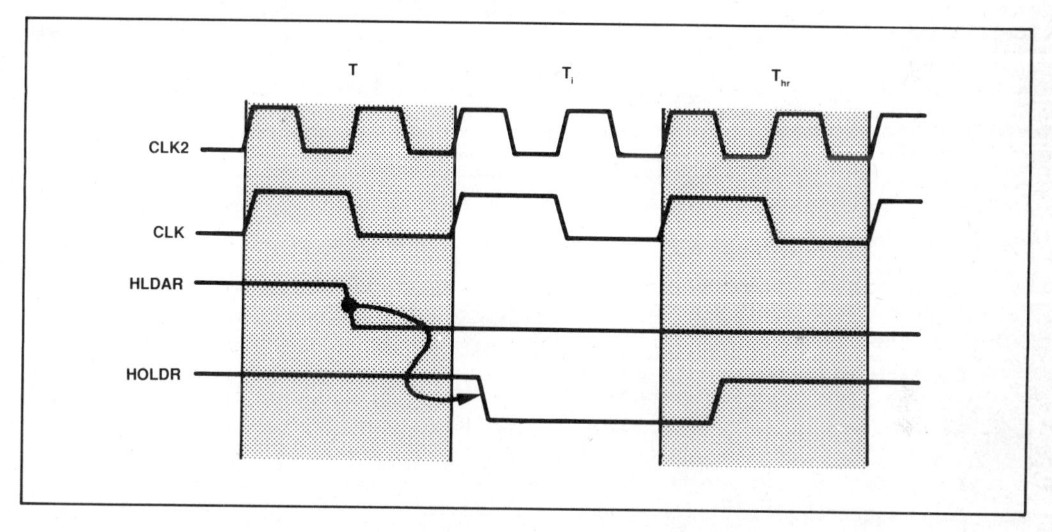

Figure 3-18: Forced Relinquishment Timing Diagram for an SBM

3.7 INTER-AGENT COMMUNICATION (IAC)

The IAC mechanism supplies 80960KB processors the capability to send and receive messages to one another and to other bus agents. The IAC mechanism functions as a non-maskable interrupt with pre-defined service routines. The 80960KB processor includes these routines to perform control functions such as purging the instruction cache, setting breakpoint registers, or stopping and starting the processor. Using IAC messages, external devices can remotely control the 80960KB. This allows easy integration of the 80960KB into system environments.

IAC messages can also generate interrupts that behave exactly as hard-wired interrupts. Since the IAC message encodes the interrupt vector, the processor can invoke any of 248 possible interrupt service routines. For further information on IAC message definitions, refer to the *80960KB Programmer's Reference Manual.*

3.7.1 Overview of IAC Operations

Figure 3-19 shows a typical example of an IAC operation. In this case, an external processor gains control of the 80960KB with an IAC operation. The external processor performs two functions: it writes the message in the message buffer, and it asserts the $\overline{\text{IAC}}$ pin of the 80960KB processor. When the processor receives the $\overline{\text{IAC}}$ signal, it stops executing its current process and performs a four-word burst read of the message buffer. After completing the read operation, the 80960KB processor automatically performs a one-word write operation to a pre-defined address to acknowledge the receipt of the message. The processor then performs the required action.

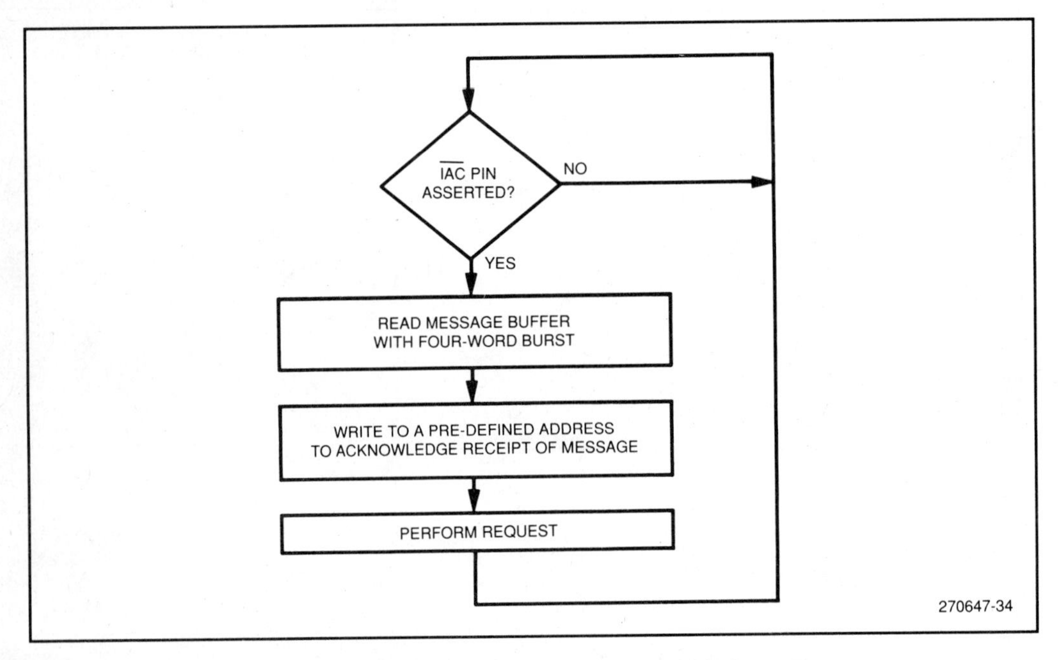

Figure 3-19: Example Flow Chart for an IAC Operation

3.7.2 IAC Messages

The IAC messages are specifically defined and behave much like machine instructions. The 80960KB processor reserves the upper 16M bytes $FF000000_{16}$ to $FFFFFFFF_{16}$ of the 4M-byte address range for IAC message operations. There are two types of messages: internal and external. Internal IAC messages allow a program to send a command to its own processor. An internal IAC message is sent by writing to address $FF000010_{16}$. Internal IAC messages cause no L-bus activity.

A program can generate External IAC messages to send a command to another processor on the L-bus or to a remote processor. A processor sends an external IAC message by writing to a buffer area and causing the pin of the receiving 80960KB to assert. Following this, the recipient processor reads the reserved address to fetch the data from its IAC message buffer. After reading the IAC message buffer, the recipient does a write operation to another reserved address to acknowledge receipt of the IAC message. The pin becomes inactive as a result of this write operation, and the processor is ready to receive another IAC.

3.7.3 Hardware Requirements for External IAC Messages

To use the external IAC feature of the 80960KB, the design requires the following: a four-word Message Buffer RAM which maps to a reserved address to store the message, IAC notification logic to assert the $\overline{\text{IAC}}$ pin of the 80960KB, and decoding logic to deassert the $\overline{\text{IAC}}$ pin on command from the 80960KB.

3.7.4 Message Buffers

Each 80960KB processor that receives an IAC message must have four 32-bit words of message buffer. This buffer uses special hardware or a reserved area in RAM. For proper operation of the buffer, two requirements must be met: the receiving 80960KB must be able to read this buffer at FF000010$_{16}$ if the receiving 80960KB's Local Processor Number (LPN) is equal to zero (see the *Reset And Initialization* section of this chapter for details ofthe LPN), or at FF000030$_{16}$ if the LPN is equal to one, and the sending processor must be able to write to this buffer.

3.7.5 $\overline{\text{IAC}}$ Pin Logic

When the IAC message buffer receives a message, IAC notification logic asserts and holds the $\overline{\text{IAC}}$ pin. After the 80960KB processor reads the IAC message, it performs a one-word write to address FF000000$_{16}$ if its LPN is zero, or FF000020$_{16}$ if its LPN is one. This reserved address serves two functions: it causes external logic to deassert the $\overline{\text{IAC}}$ pin, and it maps to a register that contains the current processor priority. If the low-order three bits of the data word have a value of 100$_{16}$ (see Figure 3-20), the external logic should deassert the $\overline{\text{IAC}}$ pin on completion of the write operation.

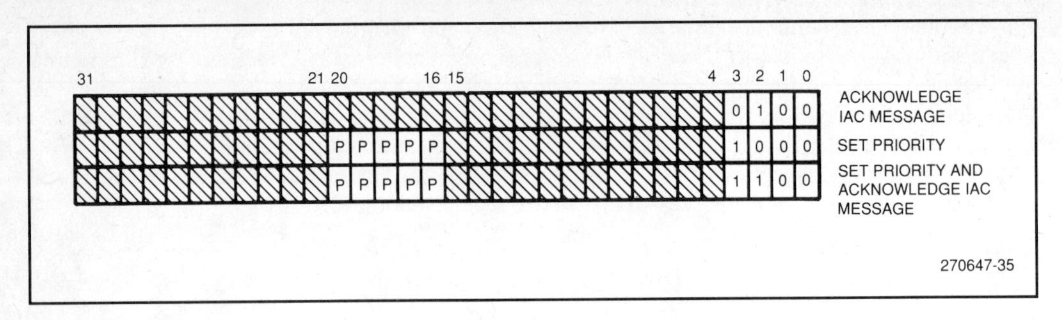

Figure 3-20: IAC Response Data

3.8 EXTERNAL PRIORITY REGISTER

The 80960KB keeps track of the current priority (a value between 0 and 31) at which it is executing. This priority indicates whether or not to service interrupts. The processor services higher priority interrupts, while it posts others for later servicing. In some system designs, it may be desirable to store the priority outside of the processor. To allow this, the 80960KB provides support for an external priority-register, which maps to address $FF000000_{16}$ if its LPN is zero, or $FF000020_{16}$ if its LPN is one. Whenever the priority of the 80960KB changes, the processor automatically updates the contents of this register (if enabled).

Two operations may help to enable this feature. If the Write External Priority bit in the PRCB is set (see the *80960KB Programmer's Reference Manual*), then the external priority register updates as a result of a process switch, an interrupt not caused by an IAC message or the execution of a MODPC instruction (modify process controls). If external IAC messages are enabled, then the external priority register updates whenever a result of an IAC changes processor priority.

3.8.1 Hardware Requirements

The 80960KB expects to write its priority into a 5-bit register mapped to address $FF000000_{16}$ if its LPN is zero, or $FF000020_{16}$ if its LPN is one. To set this priority, the processor performs a one-word write operation in the form shown in Figure 1-20. The priority is contained in bit_{20} through bit_{16}. Bit_3 is asserted to indicate that the priority is changed. It is necessary to use bit_3 as a qualifier to distinguish priority write operations from IAC message acknowledgements, which use the same reserved address. Bit_2 indicates that the IAC request signal may be de-asserted.

3.8.2 External Priority and IAC Messages

The external priority register can filter IAC messages. Since the processor always services the $\overline{\text{IAC}}$ pin (i.e., it is nonmaskable), a low-priority IAC message can interrupt a high-priority task.

To prevent this, a system can associate a priority with each IAC message. This priority is then compared to the priority stored in the external priority register and helps to decide whether or not to accept the IAC message. One way to associate a priority with an IAC message is to encode the message priority into the IAC message destination address as shown in Figure 3-21. The range of reserved addresses shown in Figure 3-21 have been set aside for this purpose.

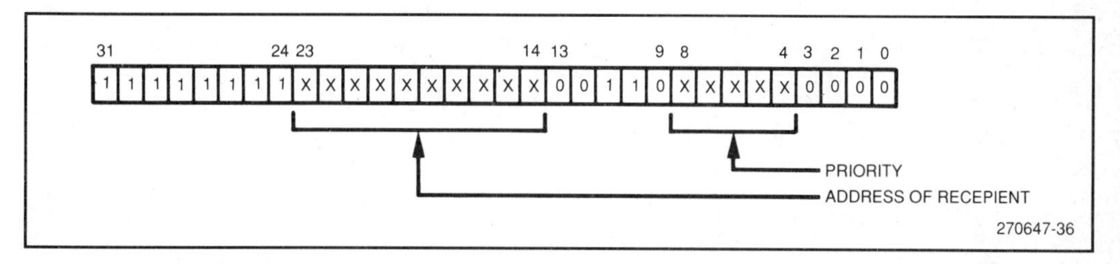

Figure 3-21: Physical Address Range for IAC Messages

3.9 INTERRUPTS

The 80960KB processor responds to external events occurring at arbitrary times through an interrupt signal. Various sources, which include hardware components and special software instructions, generate an interrupt signal that can suspend execution of the 80960KB processor's current instruction stream. This section discusses hardware-generated interrupts. For complete information on software-generated interrupts, see the *80960KB Programmers Reference Manual.*

The 80960KB architecture provides a flexible interrupt structure. The processor can be interrupted using any of the three methods shown below:

1. Receipt of a signal on any or all of the four direct interrupt input signals ($\overline{INT_0}$, INT_1, INT_2, and $\overline{INT_3}$).
2. Receipt of a signal on the interrupt request (INTR) line to obtain an external interrupt vector.
3. Receipt of an IAC message from a processor program or external source.

The setting in the on-chip Interrupt Control Register selects one of the methods. Interrupt signals can occur during any bus state regardless of the selected method.

This section provides details on the multiplexed interrupt pins, the three interrupt methods, the Interrupt Control Register, synchronization, and interrupt latency.

3.9.1 Interrupt Signals

The interrupt signals multiplex on four pins of the 80960KB processor: $\overline{INT_0}/\overline{IAC}$, INT_1, INT_2/INTR, and $\overline{INT_3}/\overline{INTA}$. The on-chip Interrupt Control register determines how the processor uses these pins (see *Interrupt Control Register* section of this chapter).

$\overline{INT_0}/\overline{IAC}$ — This pin multiplexes the **Interrupt$_0$** and **Inter-agent Communication (IAC)** request input signals. The 80960KB processor interprets this input signal as either $\overline{INT_0}$ or $\overline{IAC}$. The $\overline{INT_0}$ signal indicates a request for interrupt service. The $\overline{IAC}$ signal denotes that an IAC message is waiting.

INT_1 — The **Interrupt$_1$** input signal indicates a request for interrupt service.

$INT_2/INTR$ — This pin multiplexes the **Interrupt$_2$** and **Interrupt Request** input signals. The 80960KB processor interprets this input signal as either INT_2 or INTR. The INT_2 signal indicates a request for interrupt service. The INTR signal indicates an interrupt request from an external interrupt controller. The 80960KB processor responds with an interrupt-acknowledge sequence. To ensure an interrupt, the INTR signal must remain asserted until the first cycle of the interrupt-acknowledge transaction.

$\overline{INT_3}/\overline{INTA}$ — This pin multiplexes the **Interrupt$_3$** input signal and **Interrupt Acknowledge** output signal. The 80960KB processor uses this pin as the $\overline{INT_3}$ input signal or as the $\overline{INTA}$ output signal. The Interrupt Control Register setting selects either the combination of INTR/$\overline{INTA}$ or $INT_2/\overline{INT_3}$. The $\overline{INT_3}$ input signal indicates a request for interrupt service when it is asserted. $\overline{INTA}$ acknowledges the interrupt request from an external interrupt controller. The 80960 processor latches the $\overline{INTA}$ signal and remains valid during the T_d state and, if required, T_w states. This signal is an open-drain output.

3.9.2 Interrupt Control Register

The 80960KB processor uses a 32-bit, on-chip Interrupt Control Register to define the function of the multiplexed interrupt pins. This 32-bit Interrupt Control Register allocates eight bits for each of the four direct interrupt signals ($\overline{INT_0}$, INT_1, INT_2, and $\overline{INT_3}$). The eight bits contain the vector number for each interrupt signal, as shown in Figure 3-22. The processor automatically reads the vector number when one of the interrupt signals ($\overline{INT_0}$, INT_1, INT_2, and $\overline{INT_3}$) activates. For example, when an interrupt signals on $\overline{INT_0}$, the 80960KB processor uses bit_7-bit_0 of the Interrupt Control Register as the vector number.

The 80960KB processor uses the data field corresponding to $\overline{INT_0}$ to determine identification of the $\overline{INT_0}/\overline{IAC}$ input pin; a value of 00_{16} signifies the IAC function. If the data field corresponding to INT_2 has a value of 00_{16}, the 80960KB processor interprets the INT_2/INTR pin as the INTR input signal, and the $\overline{INT_3}/\overline{INTA}$ pin as the $\overline{INTA}$ output signal. In other words, this setting specifies that the 80960KB processor should use these two pins for communication with an external interrupt controller. When used with an external interrupt controller, the data field corresponding to INT_3 should set to FF_{16}. If the functions of INTR and $\overline{INTA}$ are selected, the direct interrupt pins $\overline{INT_0}$ and INT_1 can still be used.

The program can use Synchronous Load (synld) and Synchronous Move (synmov) instructions to read and write the on-chip Interrupt Control Register at the address $FF000004_{16}$ (see the *80960KB Programmer's Reference Manual*). The value of the data fields in the Interrupt Control Register is $FF000000_{16}$ after initialization. This setting specifies that the four interrupt pins function as $\overline{INTA}$, INTR, INT_1, and $\overline{IAC}$.

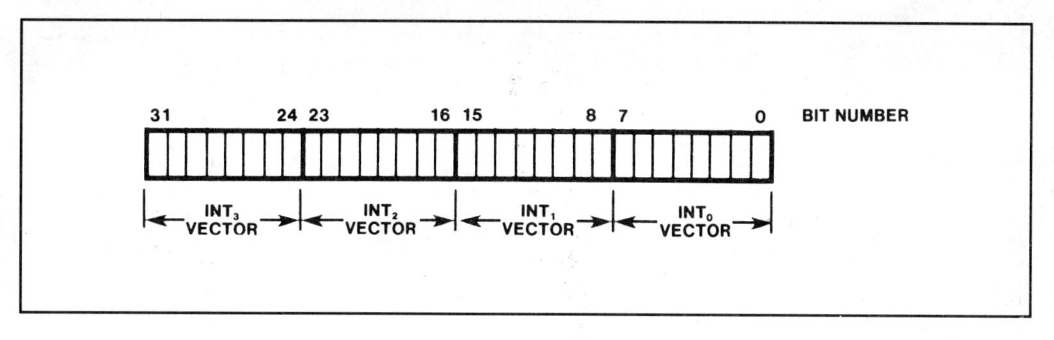

Figure 3-22: Interrupt Control Register

3.9.3 Using the Four Direct Interrupt Pins

Asserting any of the four interrupt input signals ($\overline{INT}_0$, INT_1, INT_2, $\overline{INT}_3$) will interrupt the 80960KB processor. If the signals are simultaneously asserted, the 80960KB assumes that $\overline{INT}_0$ has the highest priority, followed by INT_1, INT_2, and $\overline{INT}_3$. Software should follow this convention when programming the Interrupt Control Register. When the interrupt input signals are asserted, the 80960KB processor utilizes a vector number that the Interrupt Contro register specifies as an index to an entry in the interrupt table located in memory. For complete software information on this topic, see the *80960KB Programmer's Reference Manual.*

3.9.4 Using an External Interrupt Controller

Using the INTR and $\overline{INTA}$ signals, the 80960KB processor can perform an interrupt acknowledge sequence to communicate with an external interrupt controller. Figure 3-23 shows a timing example of an interrupt acknowledge sequence using the 8259A Programmable Interrupt Controller.

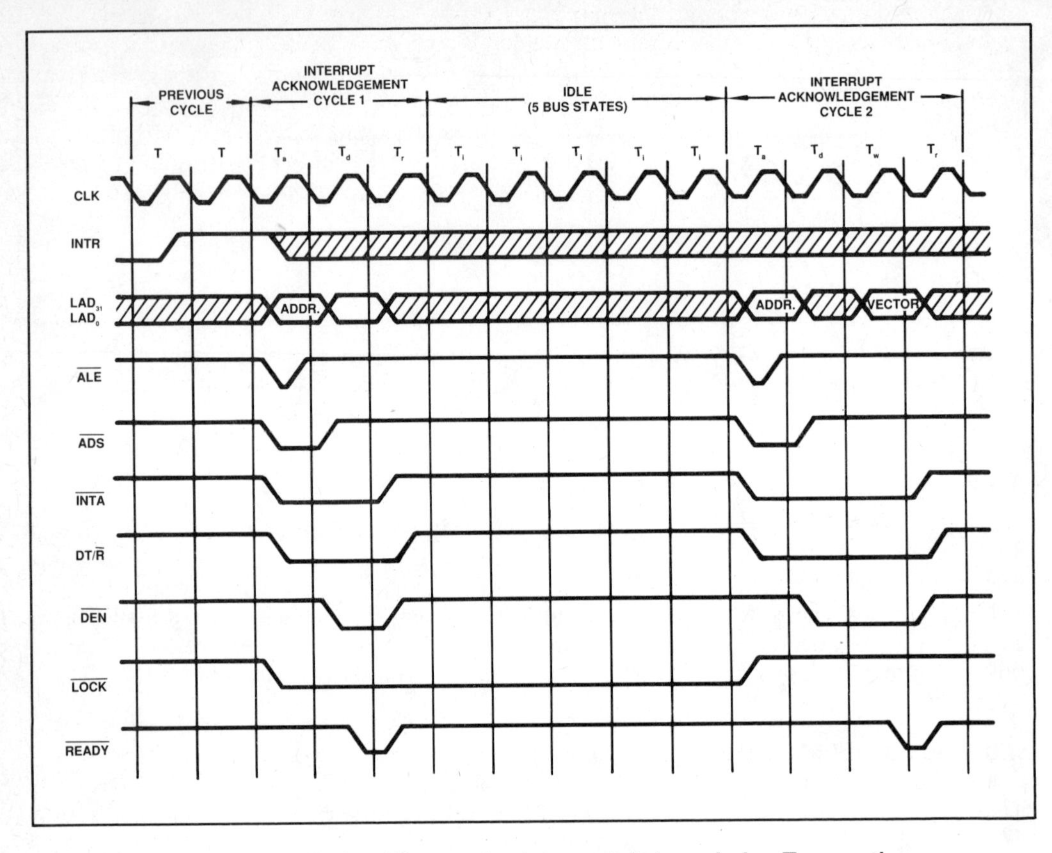

Figure 3-23: Timing Diagram for Interrupt Acknowledge Transaction

The 8259A asserts and holds INTR until the 80960KB processor activates the $\overline{\text{INTA}}$ signal for the first time. When the 80960KB processor receives an interrupt request, the CPU completes the current transaction (at some interruptible point), and asserts $\overline{\text{INTA}}$. $\overline{\text{INTA}}$ remains valid through the T_a, T_d, and T_w states. The first assertion of $\overline{\text{INTA}}$ triggers the 8259A to resolve priority among its interrupt requests.

To compensate for the timing of the 8259A, the 80960KB processor inserts five T_i states before asserting the $\overline{\text{INTA}}$ again to read the interrupt vector. Figure 1-23 shows $\overline{\text{READY}}$ asserted without a wait state during the first Interrupt Acknowledgement cycle and with one wait state during the second Interrupt Acknowledgement cycle. In practice, the 8259A would require about four wait states in both cycles. The address during the T_a state for both interrupt acknowledge cycles is $FFFFFFFC_{16}$. For more details, see the *8259A Programmable Interrupt Controller* section in Chapter 5.

The 80960KB processor services the interrupt according to its priority. If the interrupt has higher priority than the current activity, the 80960KB processor services it immediately. Otherwise, after reading the interrupt vector, the 80960KB processor posts the interrupt vector in the interrupt table. Typically, the 80960KB processor responds within 4 microseconds for an interrupt with higher priority than the current process (assuming CLK2 at 32 MHz). If the interrupt has lower priority than the current activity, the processor services the interrupt when its priority is higher than the priority of the subsequent activity of the 80960KB processor.

3.9.5 Using IAC Requests for Interrupts

An IAC can also interrupt the 80960KB processor. The 80960KB processor can use Synchronous Move instructions to send IAC messages to itself. Because this message does not utilize the L-bus when sent to the same processor, the task requires no special hardware. The *80960KB Programmer's Reference Manual* provides more details on IAC messages.

3.9.6 Synchronization

The $\overline{INT_0}$/IAC, INT_1, INT_2/INTR, and $\overline{INT_3}$ input signals are either synchronous or asynchronous to the system clock (CLK2). To properly preset the interrupt signals for synchronous operation, $\overline{INT_0/IAC}$, INT_1, INT_2/INTR, and $\overline{INT_3}$ must be deasserted for at least one processor clock cycle and asserted for at least one processor clock cycle. These signals may be deasserted and asserted individually.

If the interrupt signals are asynchronous to CLK2, the 80960KB processor internally synchronizes them. For the CPU to recognize the asynchronous interrupt input signals, the CPU must deassert them for at least two processor clock cycles, and then assert them for at least two processor clock cycles. The processor may deassert and assert the signals individually.

3.9.7 Interrupt Flows

The controller may individually assert or deassert interrupt signals. The 80960KB interrupt controller intelligently manages interrupts. Once an interrupt signal occurs, the interrupt mechanism transfers control to a microcode routine. This routine automatically allocates a new set of local registers onto the stack, posts pending interrupts, checks priorities, and suspends or aborts long instructions before executing the user's interrupt handler. Once the interrupt handler completes its tasks, the return instruction *knows* it is a return from interrupt and the 80960KB return routine restores the local, arithmetic, and process control registers, checks for pending interrupts, and returns to the next instruction of the interrupted code.

There are two main stages that the 80960KB enters before it executes the interrupt handler: hardware recognizes the interrupt and then a microcode interrupt routine executes. First, the interrupt pin is polled. Hardware stores this in a 4-bit register. The routine assigns one bit to each pin. This register captures subsequent interrupts once it recognizes one interrupt. The routine recognizes interrupts at instruction boundaries or interruptible points in long instructions (floating point). The routine immediately disables them. However, it is important to note that disabling the interrupts does *not* disable the 4-bit register. Interrupts are saved in this register until microcode reaches a point where it checks the register again. When the routine reads the register again, it clears it. The highest priority bit in the 4-bit vector clears, which indicates that the interrupt vector associated with it will be used. Then this vector is written back to the register by an ORing function within the register, thus maintaining any new interrupts that may have been signalled.

Next, the 80960KB processor recognizes an interrupt (since an event has been stored in the 4-bit register). At this point, a hardware mechanism in the interrupt controller calls the interrupt microcode routine, which executes the described action (see flow chart in Figure 3-24). After the interrupt routine completes, it calls the interrupt handler and begins executing instructions. The user supplies the routine for the interrupt handler. All the housekeeping needed to get into or out of the interrupt handler is automatically handled by the processor before the interrupt handler call; the user never needs to accomplish housekeeping activities.

The 80960KB has only one *return* instruction for all types of returns. Three bits in the *previous frame pointer* (local register 0) are known as the return status bits. These bits encode the type of call (and therefore) the type of return that occurs.

The flow diagrams show an interrupt flow, pending interrupt flow, and interrupt return flow. The 80960KB processor implements these routines in microcode.

3.9.8 Pending Interrupts

Pending interrupts occur only in three types of situations.

1. Return from interrupt, or
2. MODPC instruction (if process priority is lowered), or
3. Test pending interrupt IAC

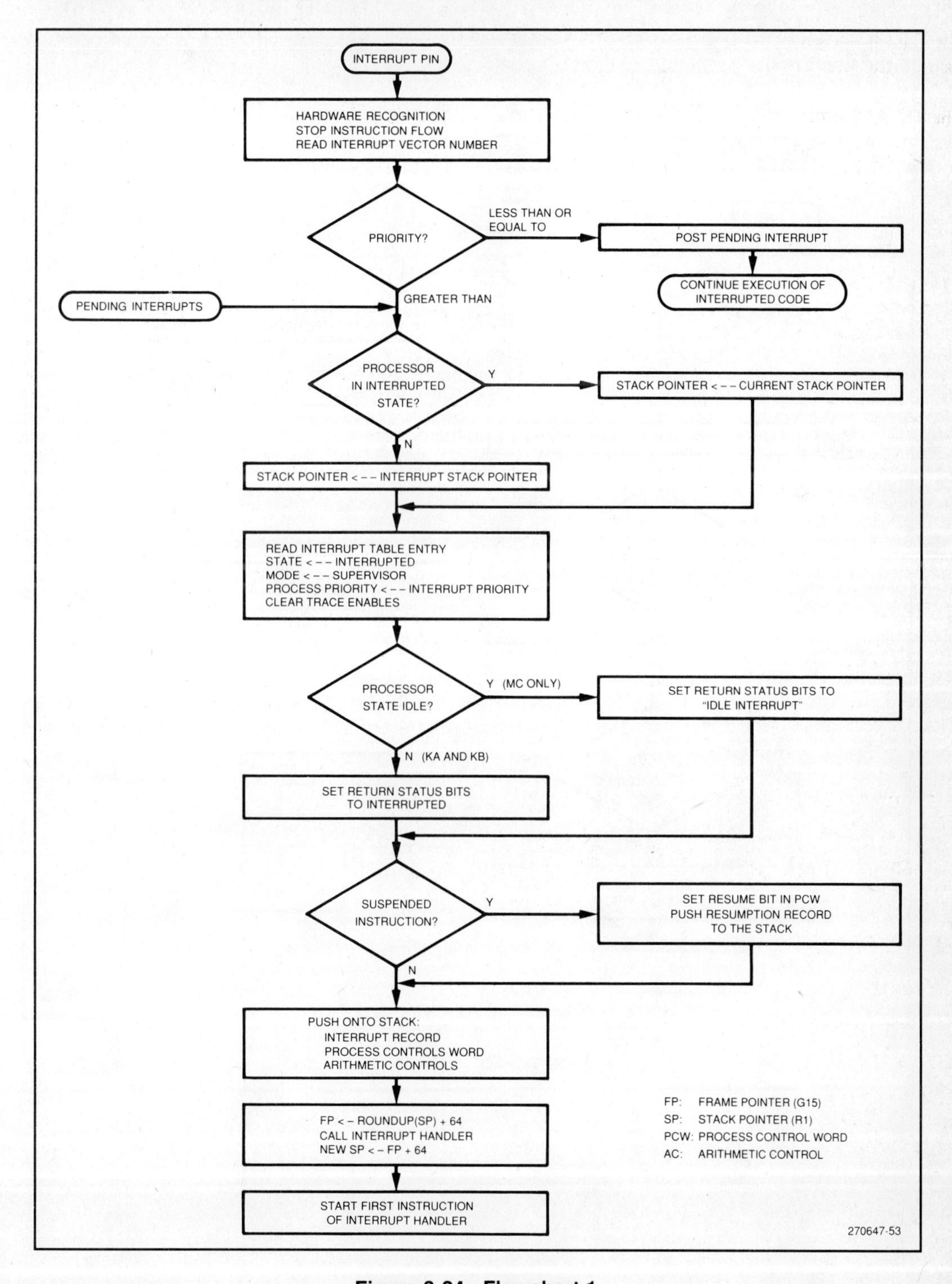

Figure 3-24: Flowchart 1

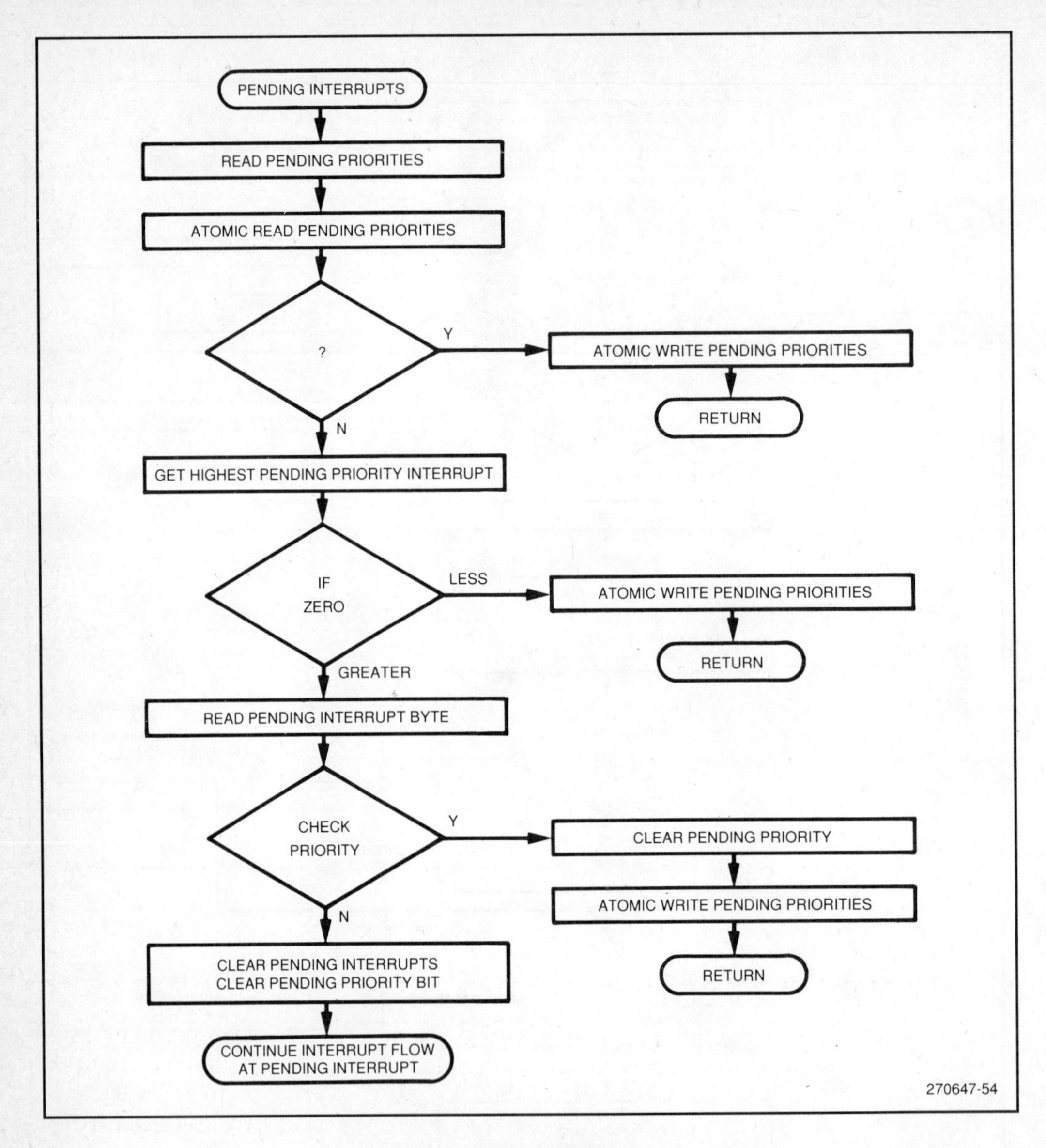

Figure 3-25: Flowchart 2

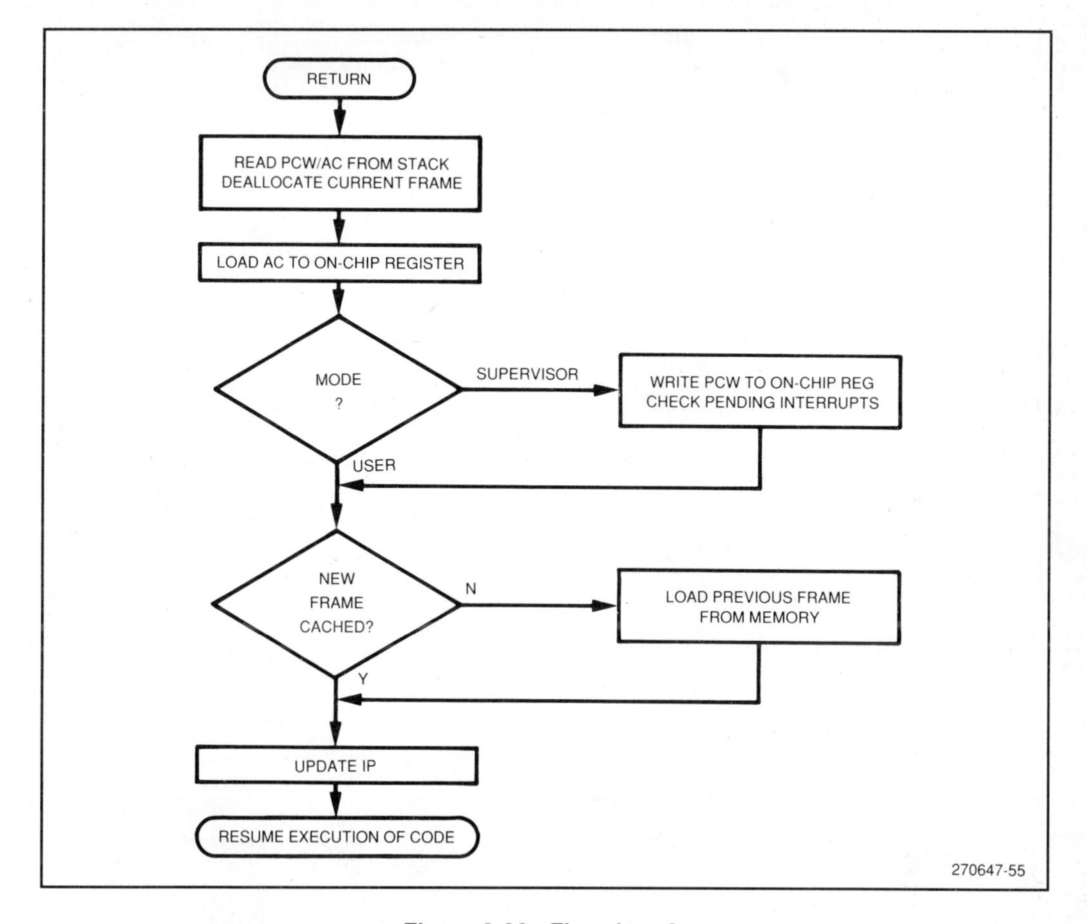

Figure 3-26: Flowchart 3

3.9.9 Interrupt Latency

The 80960KB interrupt controller manages the interrupt mechanism automatically and therefore deals with many cases. Depending on the situation, latency may vary. The interrupt latencies consist of a base latency and special case latencies added to it. These special cases consist of such things as using an 8259A interrupt controller, the local cache being full, or an interrupt occurring while the processor is already in the interrupted state.

The base interrupt latency is 85 cycles as shown in Table 3-5. Table 3-6 describes the breakdown of the base interrupt latency. Notice that it only takes 6 cycles for the 80960KB to respond to the interrupt; four cycles for hardware recognition of the interrupt, and a minimum of one cycle to respond if the interrupt occurs on an instruction boundary. The table indicates that it takes 2 cycles for interrupt signals at the beginning of a RISC instruction. This value differs depending on the instruction being interrupted and the point at which the interrupt occurs in the instruction. Table 3-7 gives values for integer execution, floating point, and transcendental floating-point instruction interrupt boundaries.

Table 3-5: Interrupt Latencies

TYPE OF LATENCY	CYCLES
Bus Interrupt Latency	85
Return	78
Interrupt immediately followed by another interrupt. Second interrupt posted to interrupt table	157
Return with a Pending Interrupt Posted	157
Pending Interrupt	0

Table 1-6: Constituent Parts of the Base Latency

CONSTITUENT LATENCIES	CYCLE
Hardware Recognition	4
Stop Current Instruction Flow Assuming a RISC Instruction	2
Determine Next IP and Save	8
Read Interrupt Vector Number	18
Check Interrupt Priority	8
Read Interrupt Table Vector	14
Check if Processor Already Interrupted	6
Save Process Control and Write Interrupt Record	10
Compute Interrupt Record address of New Local Register Set	10
Allocate New local Register Set	3
Fetch New Instruction and Start Decoding	2

Other situations that add to the latency are interrupts which signal the start of a multicycle instruction or multiple interrupts which signal at the same time. The first may cause a resumption record to store on the stack. This records all the necessary information the 80960KB needs to resume executing the interrupted instruction. Not all interruptible instructions cause a resumption record to be created. If an instruction executes for over 520 cycles, then the processor creates a resumption record. Any cycles less than that will simply restart the instruction upon return from interrupt. This provides an engineering trade-off between saving states after less than 520 cycles and restarting the instruction. Restarting the instruction requires fewer cycles (in most cases).

Table 3-7: Special Case Latencies

SPECIAL CASE LATENCIES	CYCLES
8259A Interrupt Expansion	18
Frame Cache Full	24
Current Process in "Interrupt"	14
RISC Instructions (Worst Case)	3-4
Integer Execution	10-40
Floating Point	12-96
Transcendental Floating Point	90
Instruction Cache Miss (2 Wait State)	5

Multiple interrupts signalled at various times are handled on a first come, first serve basis. Interrupts occurring at the same time are handled on a priority scheme with $\overline{INT}_3$, INT_2, INT_1, and $\overline{INT}_0$. The first interrupt is handled as soon as the 80960KB reaches an interruptible state (e.g., at an end of instruction) and subsequent interrupts are read from the interrupt control register and posted in the interrupt table as soon as the microcode routine re-enables interrupts. While interrupts are enabled, the event (another interrupt) stores in the 4-bit register as described earlier. Posting a pending interrupt to the interrupt table adds about 60 cycles to the interrupt latency. This consists of comparing the priorities of the processor and interrupt, and writing a *one* to the appropriate bits in the pending interrupt field in the interrupt table. The index vector from the interrupt control register or an 8259A vector points to the positions in the fields.

The minimum interrupt latency is 85 clocks (or 4.25 microseconds at 20 MHZ). This latency assumes the instruction handler is in the cache. If there is an instruction cache miss, five clocks for caching the instructions must be added to the base latency (assuming a two wait state memory system). In most cases, the instruction will be cached already. A program's typical latency would add about 3 more clocks for non-RISC instructions. A local register cache miss adds 24 cycles (or 1.2 microseconds) to the interrupt latency. The worst case latency would be 181 cycles (or 9.05 microseconds). This assumes the interrupt signals at the beginning of an ediv instruction (40 cycles), a local cache register miss (24 cycles) occurs, the current process is in the *interrupt* state (14 cycles), and an 8259A controller is used with 4 wait states (18 cycles).

It is important to note that during the microcode routine, all of the stack manipulations, saving state, checking priorities, and allocating new registers is accomplished automatically. When the 80960KB enters the user interrupt handler, this routine does not need to do any housekeeping chores, and it can begin immediately with useful code. The benefit is that this work is handled in microcode quickly and efficiently. Also note that the 80960KB responds to an interrupt in as little as 6 clocks. This is from the point of interrupt pin assertion to the point when the instruction flow stops and the microcode routine handles the housekeeping tasks. Normally, processors do not include any of the housekeeping activities in the interrupt latency, so care should be taken when comparing latencies. Table 3-7 lists the latencies based on special cases that occur. These values must be added to the base latency from table 3-5.

3.10 RESET AND INITIALIZATION

The system RESET signal provides an orderly way to start or restart the 80960KB processor. When the 80960KB processor detects the low-to-high transition of RESET, it terminates all external activities and places the output pins in the high-impedance state or deasserted condition. When the RESET signal falls low again, the 80960KB processor begins the initialization process and later begins fetching instructions from a specific address.

3.10.2 RESET Timing Requirements

To properly reset the 80960KB processor to a known state, the processor must receive the low-to-high transition of RESET relative to any rising edge of CLK2 and remain high for at least 41 CLK2 cycles (see Figure 3-27) RESET must be deasserted after the rising edge of CLK2, but prior to the next rising edge of CLK2. This establishes the next rising edge of CLK2 as edge A.

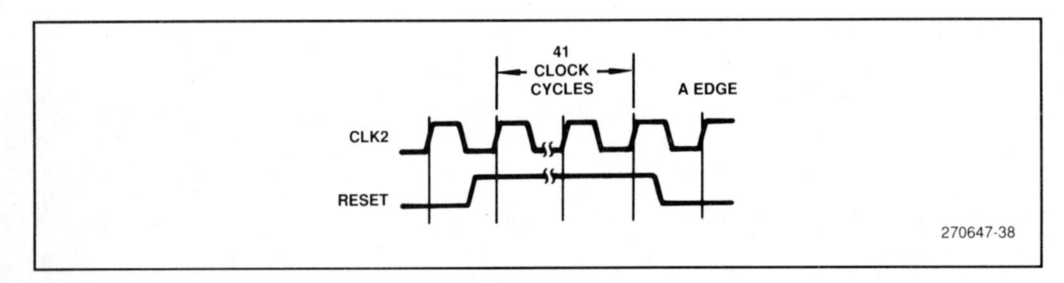

Figure 3-27: RESET Timing Diagram

3.10.3 RESET Timing Generation

Figure 3-28 illustrates a typical synchronization circuit comprised of two D-type flip-flops. This circuitry generates the RESET input signal to the 80960KB processor.

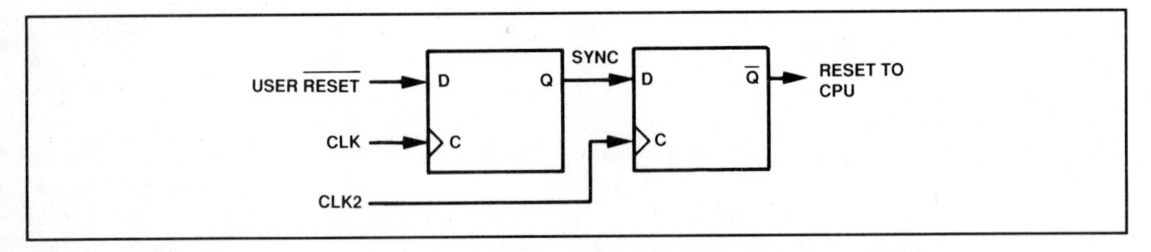

Figure 3-28: Asynchronous RESET Circuit

The timing diagram for these signals is shown in Figure 3-29. CLK or CLK2 can be used instead of CLK in Figure 3-29.

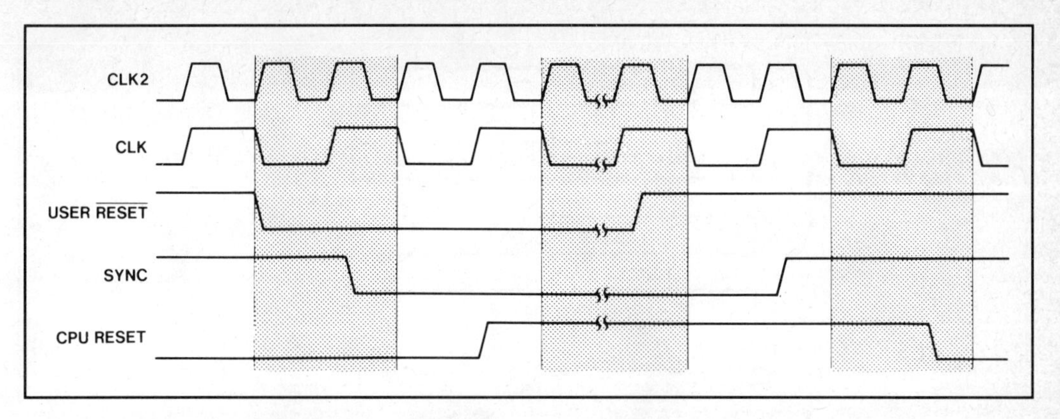

Figure 3-29: Timing Diagram for RESET Generation

3.10.4 Initialization

Figure 3-30 illustrates the initialization sequence of events. When RESET is deasserted after a minimum of 41 CLK cycles, several actions occur: the processor samples two input pins, it asserts the FAILURE output signal (see next section for the pin description), and it performs the self-test.

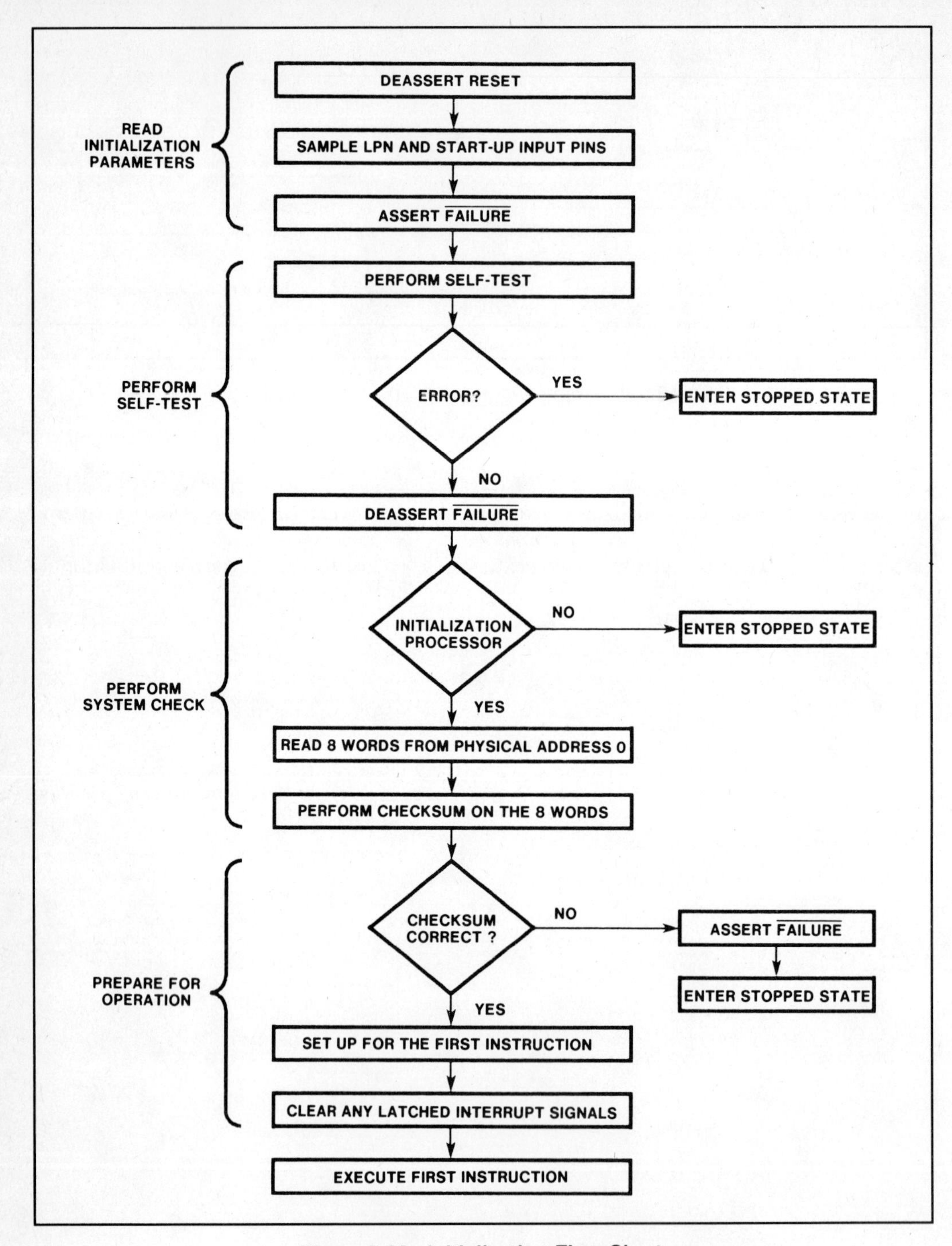

Figure 3-30: Initialization Flow Chart

When RESET is deasserted, the 80960KB processor samples the signals residing on the $\overline{INT_0}/\overline{IAC}$ and the $\overline{BADAC}$ input pins (see the next section for the pin description of $\overline{BADAC}$). At this time, these pins are interpreted as the Local Processor Number (LPN) and Startup (STARTUP) signals, respectively. A high voltage level input at the $\overline{INT_0}$ pin defines the 80960KB as the Primary Bus Master (PBM), Local Processor Number Zero (LPN0); a low voltage level defines the 80960KB as the Secondary Bus Master (SBM), Local Processor Number One (LPN1). During initialization of a uniprocessor system, the design should always assign the 80960KB as the Primary Bus Master. The STARTUP input pin indicates whether the 80960KB processor performs initialization (high voltage level) or not (low voltage level). The STARTUP signal allows the processor to perform system initialization. Figure 3-32 provides a sample circuit for driving the LPN and STARTUP signals.

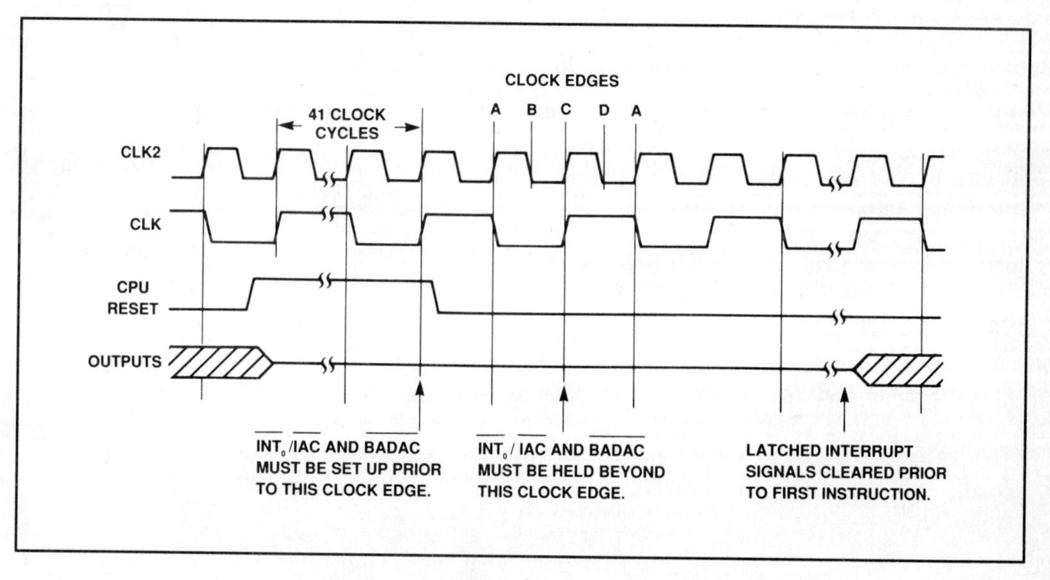

Figure 3-31: RESET Signal Timing Relationship

Besides sampling the two input pins, the 80960KB processor holds the $\overline{FAILURE}$ output signal asserted after RESET is deasserted. The $\overline{FAILURE}$ signal remains asserted while the CPU performs the self-test. If the processor detects a failure during the self-test, $\overline{FAILURE}$ remains asserted and the CPU enters the stopped state where the processor does nothing. At this time, all outputs from the 80960KB will be disabled (high-impedance or deasserted). If the self-test completes successfully, the CPU deasserts the $\overline{FAILURE}$ signal.

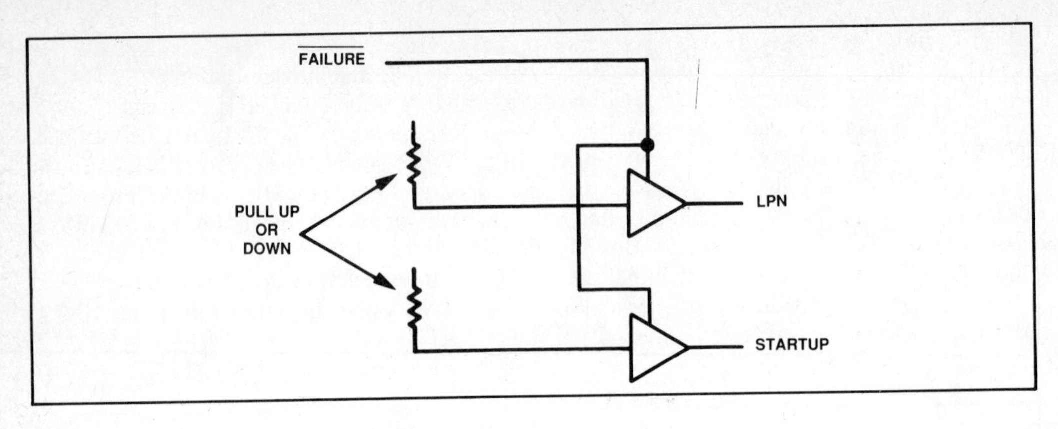

Figure 3-32: Initialization Circuitry

An 80960KB processor designated as the initialization processor proceeds with a checksum test of eight words fetched from memory at physical address $0000\ 0000_{16}$. This ensures that the memory and L-bus operate correctly. If the checksum is incorrect, the FAILURE signal is reasserted and the 80960KB processor enters the stopped state. After a successful checksum test, the 80960KB processor uses some of the previously fetched words as addresses to initial data structures. The *80960KB Programmer's Reference Manual* provides complete details. Just prior to executing the first instruction, the 80960KB processor clears any latched interrupt signals.

3.11 ERROR SIGNALS

The 80960KB processor incorporates an input signal (BADAC) for notification of an error condition in the system, and provides an output signal (FAILURE) for notification of an error within the processor.

BADAC — The Bad Access input signal indicates to the processor that an error occurred during the current data transfer. If the system asserts BADAC after a Synchronous Move or Synchronous Load instruction, the error is recoverable. The 80960KB processor samples the BADAC input signal during the cycle following the last assertion of the READY signal (state t_r).

FAILURE — The FAILURE signal indicates that an error occurred during initialization. The 80960KB processor always asserts FAILURE after the activation of the RESET signal. If the processor detects a failure during a self-test, FAILURE remains asserted. Otherwise, the processor deasserts FAILURE after performing a successful self-test. If the initial memory checksum is incorrect, the initialization process reasserts FAILURE a second time, and holds it active. FAILURE is an open-drain output signal.

3.12 80960KB SELF-TEST

The 80960KB Processor implements an automatic self-test following the receipt of any system RESET command. Before any bus activity occurs, the processor executes enough self-checking tasks to guarantee the proper operation of 50 percent of its internal logic, including the following major component blocks:

- Instruction Fetch Unit (IFU)
- Integer Execution Unit (IEU)
- Micro-Instruction Sequencer (MIS)

This section describes the action of the on-chip self-test logic as it tests the above logic.

3.12.1 Scope of Self-Test

The self-test directly tests or indirectly tests the elements of the 80960KB components below.

- Directly tests:
  - Micro-instruction ROM and control Logic
  - Instruction Fetch Unit Cache
  - Instruction Execution Unit RAM Array and Literals
- Indirectly Tests:
  - Access to the Micro-instruction Bus
  - Access to the Data Bus.
  - Control logic and data paths of the Micro-instruction Sequencer, the Instruction Execution Unit, and the Instruction Fetch Unit.

The test does not check the Instruction Decoder Logic, the Floating-point unit nor the IFU Instruction Pointer and its fetch and control logic.

3.12.2 Test Algorithm and Operation

Before the test begins, the 80960KB processor tri-states its local bus drivers. The processor then uses a checksum method to compare expected data and actual data results. If the test encounters a failure at any point, the processor asserts the $\overline{\text{FAILURE}}$ signal to notify the system.

The test performs its test algorithm with the following sequence.

1. Write data to the Integer Execution Unit (IEU) and the Instruction Fetch Unit (IFU). Then, verify the integrity of data with read instructions. This task follows the sequence below:

- Write the IEU.
- Write the IFU.
- Read the data written to the IEU RAM array and literals.
- Read the data written to the IFU Cache.

2. Repeat the process above.
3. Read the Microinstruction Sequencer ROM and compare the actual results with the expected results.

3.13 SUMMARY

The L-bus is a high-speed 32-bit multiplexed bus with burst transfer capability and is designed to operate with the high-performance 80960KB processor. The L-bus consists of two signal groups: address/data, and control. The 80960KB processor uses these signal groups to perform read, write, and burst transactions.

The arbitration, interrupt, and reset operations relate to the L-bus transactions. The arbitration operation transfers control of the L-bus to another bus master. Three methods are available to handle interrupts: invoking the on-chip interrupt controller, employing an external interrupt controller using the INTR/$\overline{\text{INTA}}$ signals, or with IAC messages. The reset function sets the 80960KB processor to a known internal state after it successfully completes the self-test. These operations offer power and flexibility to hardware system design using the 80960KB processor.

This chapter focuses on the L-bus and its relationship with the 80960KB processor. The next two chapters develop guidelines on interfacing memory and peripheral devices into the L-bus hardware system.

Memory Interface 4

CHAPTER 4
MEMORY INTERFACE

The high-speed L-bus architecture includes many features that enhance high-performance designs. In particular, the burst-transfer feature allows up to four successive 32-bit data word transfers at a maximum rate of one word every processor clock cycle. This chapter outlines approaches for memory designs that use these features, describes memory design considerations, analyzes the timing, and lists a number of useful examples. The examples provide concepts that apply to a wide variety of memory system implementations.

4.1 BASIC MEMORY INTERFACE

Figure 4-1 shows the major logic blocks of the memory interface circuit. The data transceivers buffer the data to compensate for bus loading. They also compensate for any slow devices that may connect to the 80960KB processor. The Address Latches demultiplex the address/data signals from the 80960KB processor and latch the address. The address decoder selects the appropriate memory device from the latched address. To accommodate a memory burst transaction, the burst logic decrements the word count, increments the local address lines 3 and 2 (LAD_3 and LAD_2), and generates a CYCLE-IN-PROGRESS signal. The byte enable latch stores the byte enable signals. The timing control generates a $\overline{\text{READY}}$ signal and other specific signals that a particular memory device would require.

Although not part of the basic memory interface, Figure 4-1 includes the DRAM controller, SRAM interface, DRAM, SRAM, and EPROM. A hardware system design typically places the DRAM, SRAM, and EPROM in separate subsystems.

Although the memory interface circuit may use programmable logic, gate arrays, or other custom logic, the examples here use standard components wherever possible to illustrate design concepts.

4.1.1 Data Transceivers

The 80960KB address/data bus can directly drive large capacitive loads eliminating the need for data bus transceivers in many systems. Data bus transceivers are necessary whenever DC loads exceed data sheet specifications or whenever additional delays due to capacitive loading exceed the additional propagation delay of a transceiver.

The 80960KB capacitive derating curve shown in the data sheet provides a derating of about one nS per 15 pF of additional load. A FAST transceiver has a typical delay of about five nS plus a capacitive derating of about one nS per 50 pF. Using these values, the crossover point would occur at 160 pF. Consideration must also be given to reflections due to long board traces. The design should use transceivers with lower capacitive loads if the address/data bus is to be terminated resistively.

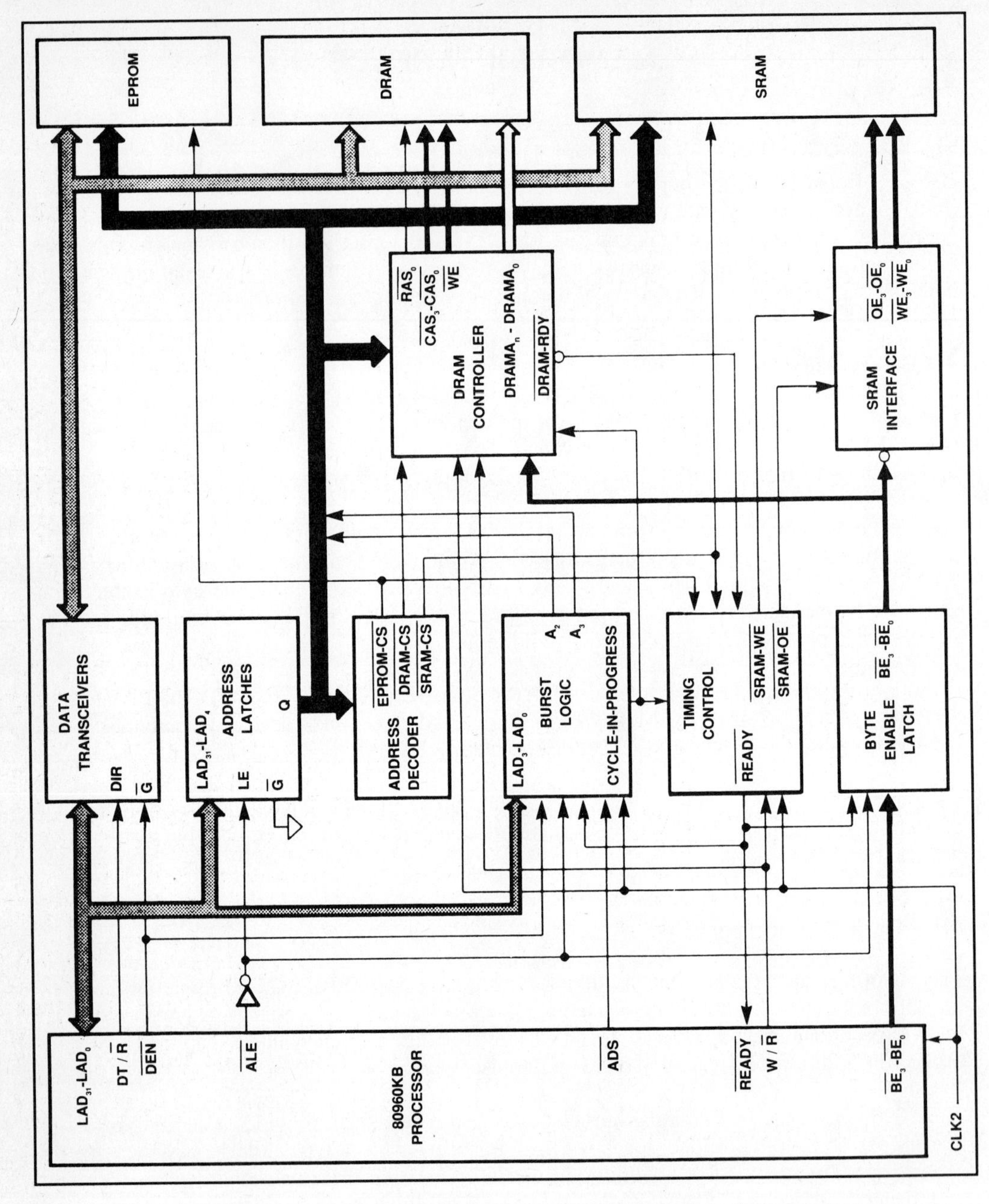

Figure 4-1: Simplified Block Diagram for Memory Interface Logic

Figure 4-2 shows a sample circuit that uses data transceivers for the 80960KB processors. The processor supplies DT/R to control transceiver direction and DEN to control output enables.

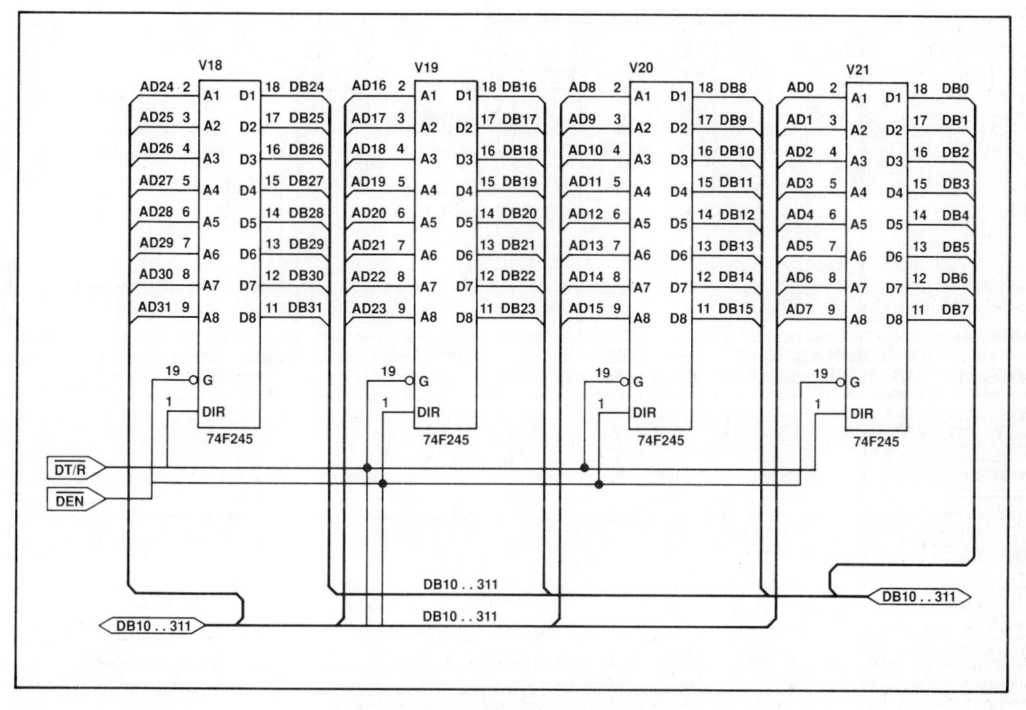

Figure 4-2: Data Transceivers

Standard 8-bit transceivers provide isolation and additional drive capability for the L-bus. Transceivers can prevent bus contention that can occur if some memories are slow to remove data from the L-bus after a read operation. For example, if a write operation follows a read operation, the 80960KB processor may drive the L-bus before a slow device removes its output data, potentially causing a current spike on the power and ground lines. The design can omit transceivers, however, if the data float time of the device is short enough and the load does not exceed the 80960KB device specifications.

4.1.2 Address Latch/Demultiplexer

Conventional transparent latches can demultiplex the address/data lines of the 80960KB processor and hold the address constant during a memory operation. The $\overline{\text{ALE}}$ signal from the 80960KB processor controls the latch. $\overline{\text{ALE}}$ passes through an inverter such that when $\overline{\text{ALE}}$ goes low, the address flows through the latch. You can use the low-to-high transition of $\overline{\text{ALE}}$ to latch the address. The burst logic latches the lower four address lines (LAD_3 - LAD_0).

Figure 4-3 shows a sample circuit that uses 74F373 transparent latches for address latching. Since the 74F373's require a non-inverted latch enable signal, the design inverts $\overline{\text{ALE}}$ through a NAND gate.

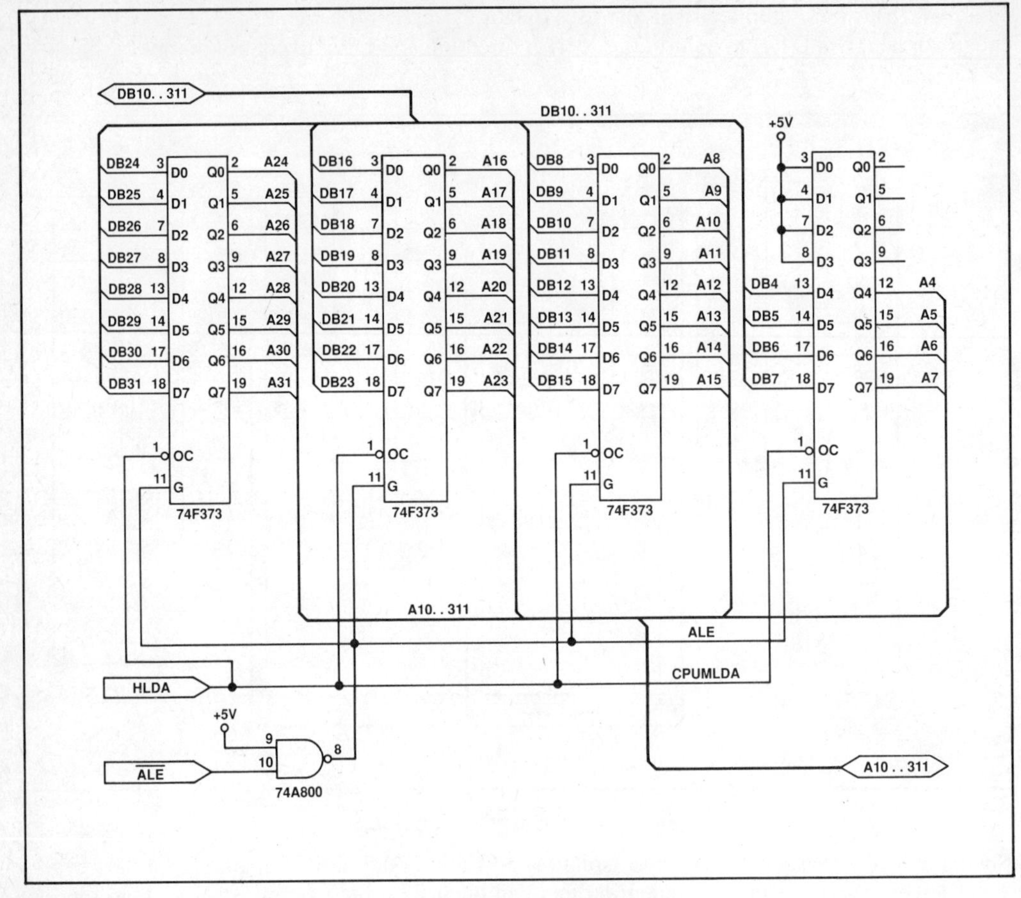

Figure 4-3: Address Latching

If the circuit design uses multiple bus masters (such as an 80960KB and an 82380), the hold acknowdedge (HLDA) from the processor should connect to the address latch output controls to tri-state the address latches (when the processor is not the bus master). Whenever the processor is the bus master, it pulls HLDA low to turn on the address latch drivers. When the processor relinquishes bus ownership, it drives HLDA high which then disables the address latch drivers. In a design with a single bus master, the address latches can be left enabled.

4.1.3 Address Decoder

The 80960KB processor accesses both memory and I/O devices when it supplies a 32-bit address and a read/write command. The address decoder selects a particular memory or I/O device when it decodes the address lines. The following discussion focuses on memory selection. The *Address Decoder* section in Chapter 5 discusses I/O device selection using memory-mapped I/O techniques.

The memory address can be divided into regions with one region dedicated to EPROM or ROM, another to RAM, and another to the I/O registers. In a 80960KB-based system, the

ROM address space is likely to begin at address $0000\ 0000_{16}$ because the CPU begins execution at this address. The RAM or I/O regions can begin at any other address in the 4G-byte address range except for addresses $FF000000_{16}$ through $FFFFFFFF_{16}$, which the 80960KB processor reserves for interagent communication. Typically, the processor decodes the higher-order address bits to develop enable signals for ROM, RAM, and I/O devices.

You can place the address decoder either before or after the address latches. Usually, it is placed after the latches so that the chip select signal does not need to be latched.

4.1.4 Chip Select Generation

Most memory and peripheral devices use a 3-line control system with a chip select signal to enable the device, an output control signal to enable device reads, and a write strobe signal to clock data into the device on writes. In addition, the design usually provides address inputs to select areas within the device (see Figure 4-4).

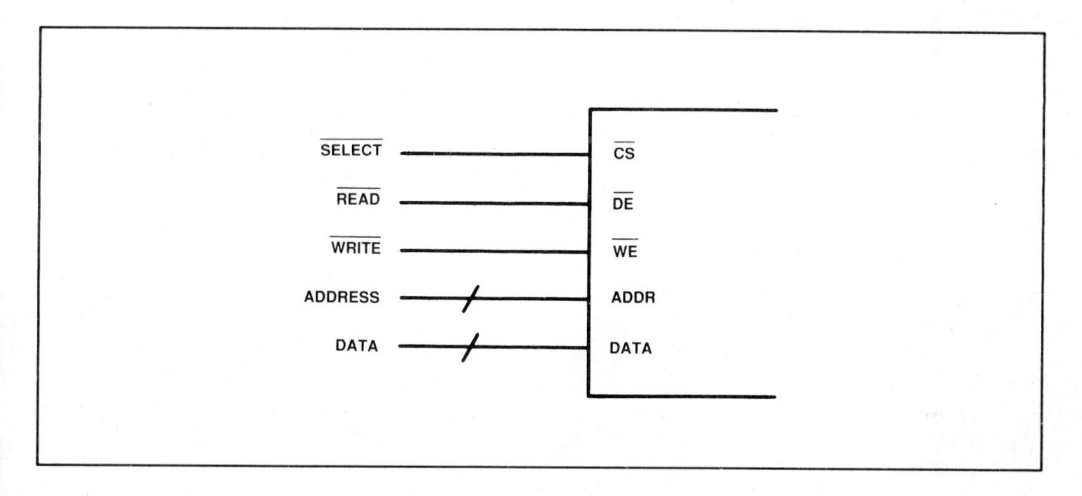

Figure 4-4: Input Control Circuitry

The speed with which a circuit can generate chip select signals can determine access device timing. Care must be taken to minimize address and chip select generation delays in order to achieve optimum bus performance. Figure 4-5 shows sample chip select logic. This design uses a standard 74F138 3-to-8 line decoder to generate chip selects. The total delay path from the start of a bus cycle to valid chip selects consists of the output valid delay of the 80960KB, T_{cd}; the propagation delay of the 74F373 address latches; and the propagation delay of the 74F138:

$$\text{Chip Select Delay} = T_{cd} + T_{prop\text{-}F373} + T_{prop\text{-}F138}$$

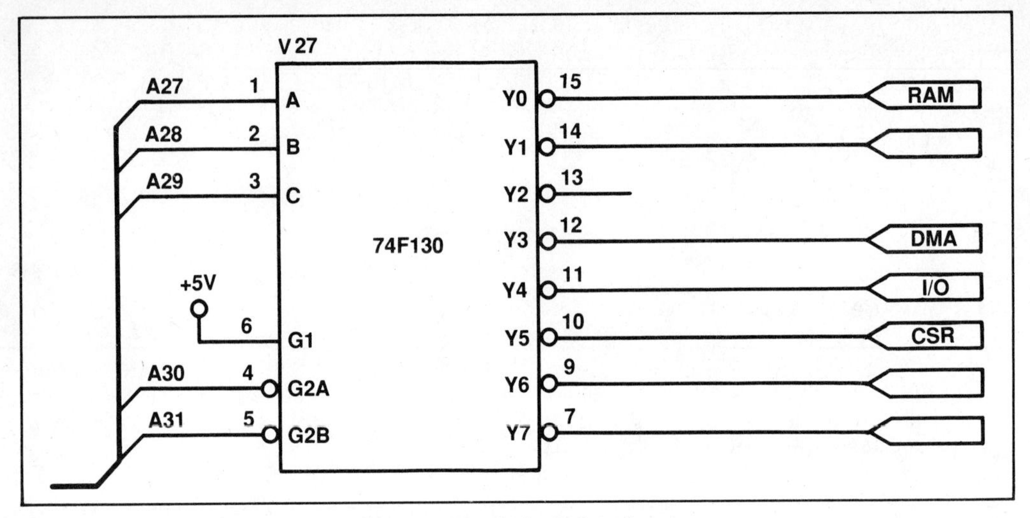

Figure 4-5: Chip Select Logic

Assuming a 25 MHz 80960KB and using the values for worst case data sheet specifications for the TTL parts, the chip select delay formula results in a total of 44 nS from the beginning of the bus address cycle, T_a. At a system frequency of 25 MHz (40 nS clock period), this translates into 4 nS for the first data cycle (T_d). In a typical design, the lower two bits of the address are not valid until about 7 nS (assuming D-speed PALS) into the first T_d cycle. In this case, the bus is address delay limited and the resulting chip select delay is more than adequate.

4.1.5 Burst Logic

To enhance system performance, the 80960KB processor performs burst transactions that transfer up to four data words at a maximum rate of one word every clock cycle. You can use the static column mode or nibble mode features of the DRAM (see the *DRAM Controller* section of this chapter) to take advantage of the burst transfer capability of the DRAM controller.

The burst logic operates with EPROM, SRAM, or DRAM memories. Because the 80960KB processor ensures that a burst transaction cannot exceed four words or cross a 16-byte boundary, incrementing LAD_3 and LAD_2 after a single data word transfer makes the burst transfer transparent to the memory devices. Intel's 85C960 Programmable Logic Device can provide chip select, wait-state generation, and burst timing for the 80960KB.

Figure 4-6 shows the flow chart for the burst logic. If $\overline{ADS}$ is low and $\overline{DEN}$ is high, then the burst logic latches LAD_3 through LAD_0. The burst logic checks the SIZE signals (LAD_1 and LAD_0). If the value of the SIZE signals equal zero, then the burst logic initiates on memory cycle and terminates. If the value of the SIZE signals do not equal zero, the burst logic runs one memory cycle, increments the lower two latched addresses (A2 and A3), and decrements the SIZE value. The burst logic then checks the value of the SIZE signals again.

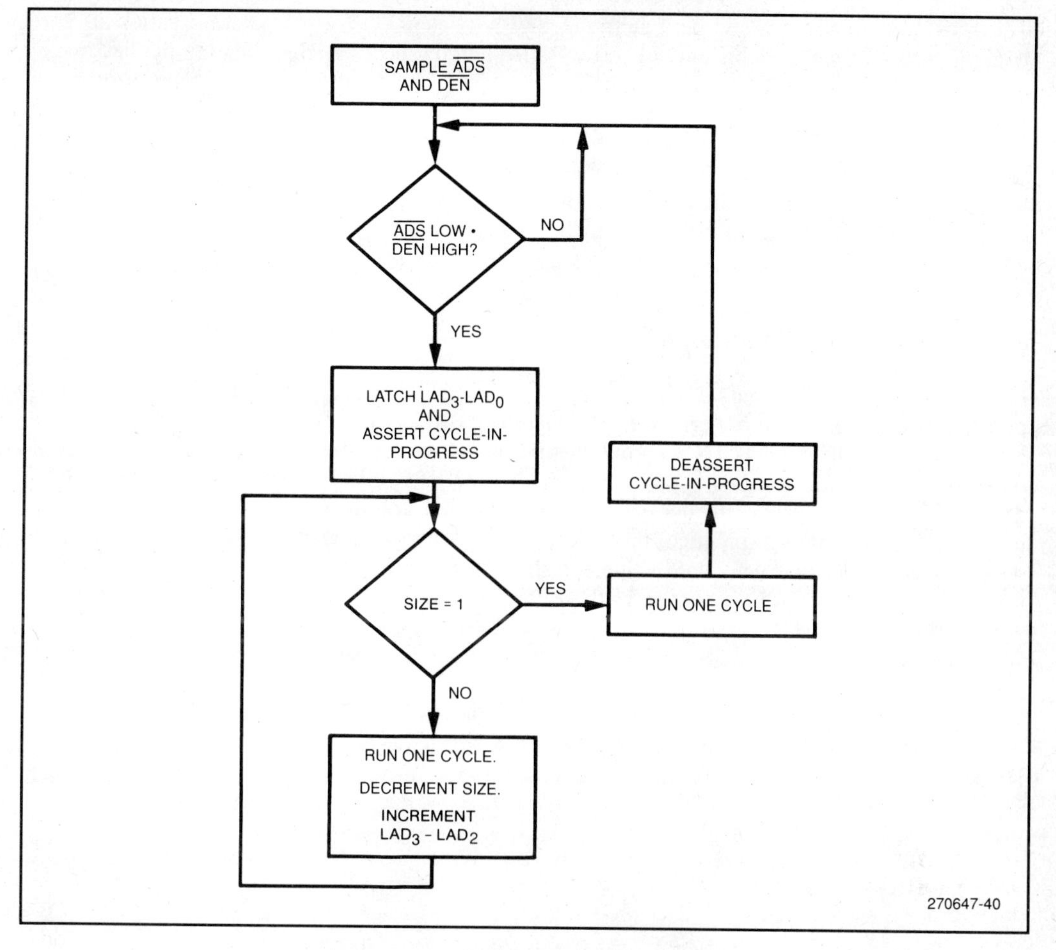

Figure 4-6: Burst Logic Flow Chart

The 80960KB processors use a burst bus which requires a small amount of external support logic. A 2-bit counter supplies the lower two bits of address for a 4-word burst. Another 2-bit counter decrements the number of cycles remaining in the burst. Bus command logic generates the required read and write command signals for various peripheral components. Most systems use ready generation logic to insert wait states for slow memory devices and peripheral components.

The Address Up-Counter supplies the lower two bits of address which change during the burst cycle. The initial count value loads from the processor's LAD_2 and LAD_3 lines. The counter then increments on an *A* CLK2 edge with the assertion of $\overline{READY}$.

The Burst Down Counter generates a signal called BURST that marks the last cycle of a burst access. This signal, along with $\overline{READY}$ marks the beginning of a T_r cycle. During T_r, all devices must exit the bus. In most designs, synchronous output enables control most devices.

The programmable logic devices generating the output enables must therefore anticipate the beginning of a T_r cycle. This is marked by BURST being deasserted, indicating the last cycle of an access, and by $\overline{READY}$ asserted, indicating the last clock of the cycle. In designs where all output enables are asynchronously derived from the processor's W/$\overline{R}$ and $\overline{DEN}$ signals, the Burst Down Counter may not be needed. The Burst Down Counter functions in exactly the same manner as the Address Up Counter except that it decrements on *A* CLK2 edges when $\overline{READY}$ is asserted. It is loaded with an initial burst length count from LAD_0 through LAD_1 during the T_a cycle and decrements at the end of subsequent T_d or T_w cycles when $\overline{READY}$ is asserted.

4.1.6. Burst Ready Generation

Interfacing the 80960KB burst bus to devices which need more access time than a single CLK1 period requires the use of a Burst Ready Generator (BRG). The BRG inserts wait states into each data cycle of a burst. To accomplish this, it delays the assertion of $\overline{READY}$ until the occurrence of a predetermined number of CLK1's. The BRG differs from a conventional single data cycle ready generator in that each cycle of a burst could theoretically have a different number of wait states. In practice, this is not usually the case. Most memory and peripheral devices have either one wait state value for all cycles in a burst (e.g., 2, 2, 2, 2) or differing numbers of wait states for the first and subsequent cycles (e.g., 2, 1, 1, 1).

Some designs may also require differing wait state counts for read and write operations (e.g., 1, 0, 0, 0 reads and 1, 1, 1, 1 writes. In addition, different memory and peripheral devices require different numbers of wait states. The BRG must therefore decide how many wait states to insert based on which device is accessed. Figure 4-7 provides a block diagram for an example BRG.

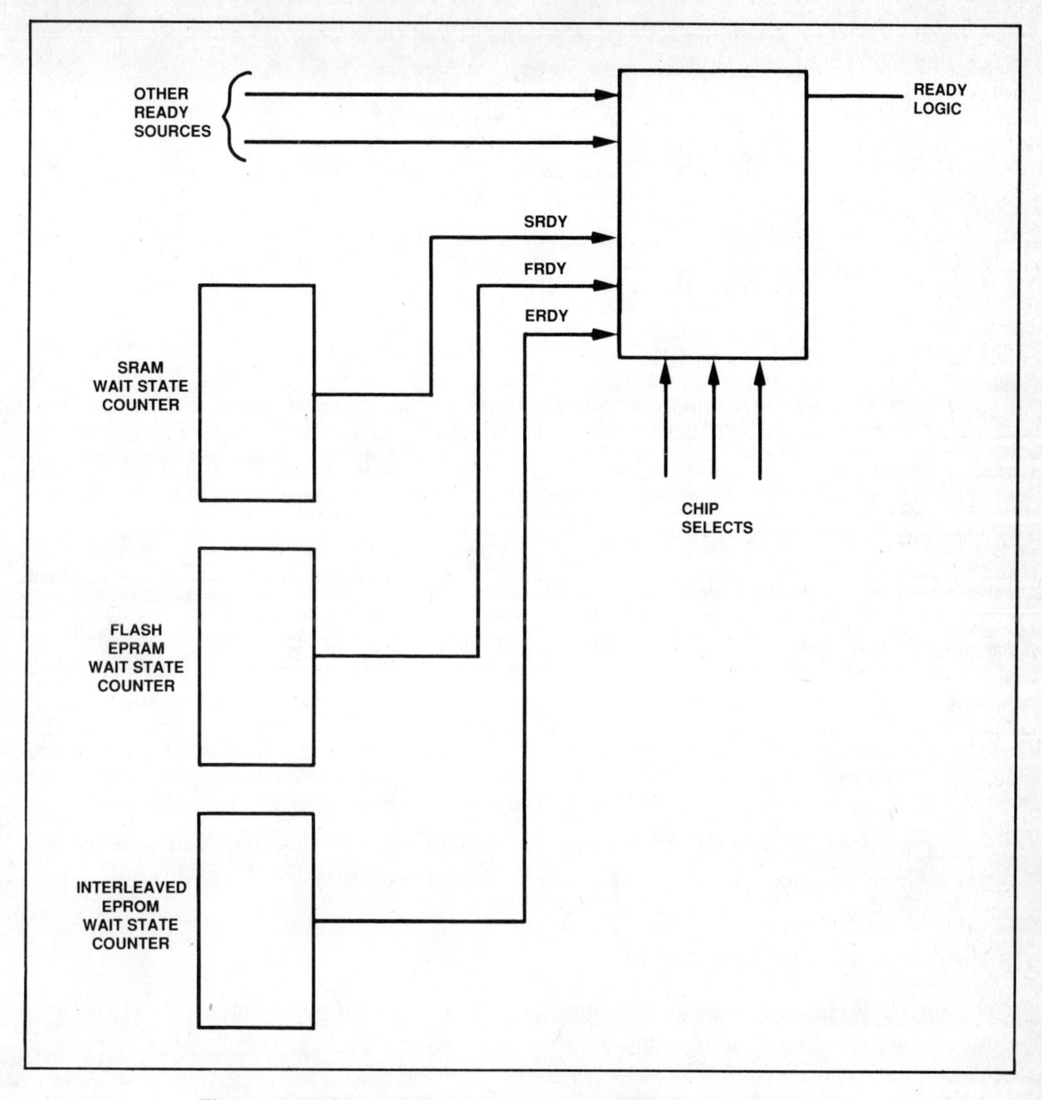

Figure 4-7: Burst Ready Generator (BRG) Block Diagram

4.1.7 Byte Enable Latch

The byte enable latch holds the byte enable signals constant until the DRAM controller or SRAM interface uses the signals.As mentioned in the *L-Bus Signal Groups* section in Chapter 3, the byte enable signals specify which bytes (up to four) on the 32-bit data bus transfer during the data cycle.Each individual byte enable signal selects eight data lines (see Table4-1).

Table 4-1: Byte Enable Signal Decoding

Byte Enable Signal	Date Line Selection
$\overline{BE}_0$	LAD_7-LAD_0
$\overline{BE}_1$	LAD_{15}-LAD_8
$\overline{BE}_2$	LAD_{23}-LAD_{16}
$\overline{BE}_3$	LAD_{31}-LAD_{24}

The byte enable outputs ($\overline{BE}_3$ - $\overline{BE}_0$) of the 80960KB processors mark which bytes on the data bus are valid (for writes) or requested (for reads). In a typical system design, the byte enable signals qualify the control inputs of various memory devices and peripheral components. During a read access, the 80960KB processors automatically select the proper bytes. In this case, external logic may ignore byte enables. During write operations for some designs, peripheral components may ignore byte enables. However, in all cases, writes to memory devices containing code or system data structures must be qualified by byte enables.

The design should pipeline byte enable outputs of the 80960KB processors. The processor asserts byte enables for the first data cycle (T_{d0}) during the address cycle (T_a). Similarly, the processor asserts byte enables for the second data cycle (T_{d1}) during the first data cycle (T_{d0}) and so on. During the last data cycle (T_{d3}), the byte enables are undefined. The processors pipeline the byte enables to ensure that they do *not* place the relatively slow assertion time of the processor's drivers in the critical timing path for memory accesses. The design uses fast external logic to latch the byte enables which allows access to the byte enables much earlier in a cycle.

You can use the $\overline{ALE}$ signal or the combination of the $\overline{ADS}$ and $\overline{DEN}$ signals to latch the first byte enable signals, and $\overline{READY}$ to latch subsequent byte enable signals for each word.

4.1.8 Bus Command Generation

Bus commands enable devices to drive the data bus during read operations or to validate data during write operations. Timing requirements for these signals vary according to the accessed device. In general, a small set of signals will handle all cases.

Bus writes for an older single-cycle microprocessor consist of asserting a write command signal at the beginning of the cycle and de-asserting it at the end of the cycle. The circuitry strobes write data into the target device on the rising edge of the de-asserting write signal. On burst bus microprocessors (such as the 80960KB), this single rising edge write signal is no longer sufficient. Each cycle within the burst needs its own rising edge. Furthermore, the fixed data to write strobe timing relationship of the older scheme did not allow for the differing timing requirements of different peripheral and memory devices. In 80960KB systems, you generate write strobes which will accurately match strobe timing to target devices.

4.2 SRAM INTERFACE

You can use the basic memory interface in conjunction with the SRAM interface to read and write to SRAM. This section describes the SRAM interface and examines the timing.

4.2.1 SRAM Interface Logic

The SRAM interface logic uses the latched byte enable signals, the $\overline{\text{SRAM-OE}}$, and the $\overline{\text{SRAM-WE}}$ signals to generate four write enable signals, SRAM-WE_3 through $\overline{\text{SRAM-WE}_0}$ (See Figure 4-8). These signals allow the 80960KB processor to write to the data byte that the byte enable signals specify. SRAMs with separate $\overline{\text{OE}}$ and $\overline{\text{CS}}$ signals require only one $\overline{\text{OE}}$ signal per bank since the 80960KB ignores unrequested bytes in read operations.

4.2.2 SRAM Timing Considerations

This section analyzes the critical timing paths of the SRAM control signals. From the critical path, timing equations determine the memory access time for no-wait state operations.

When evaluating critical timing paths, the timing calculations should use worst-case data sheet parametric specifications rather than typical specifications. By using worst-case timing values, the design assures reliable operation over all variations in temperature, voltage, and individual device characteristics. To determine these timing values, you should assume the maximum propagation delay to latch an address, select a memory device, and pass information through data buffers and transceivers.

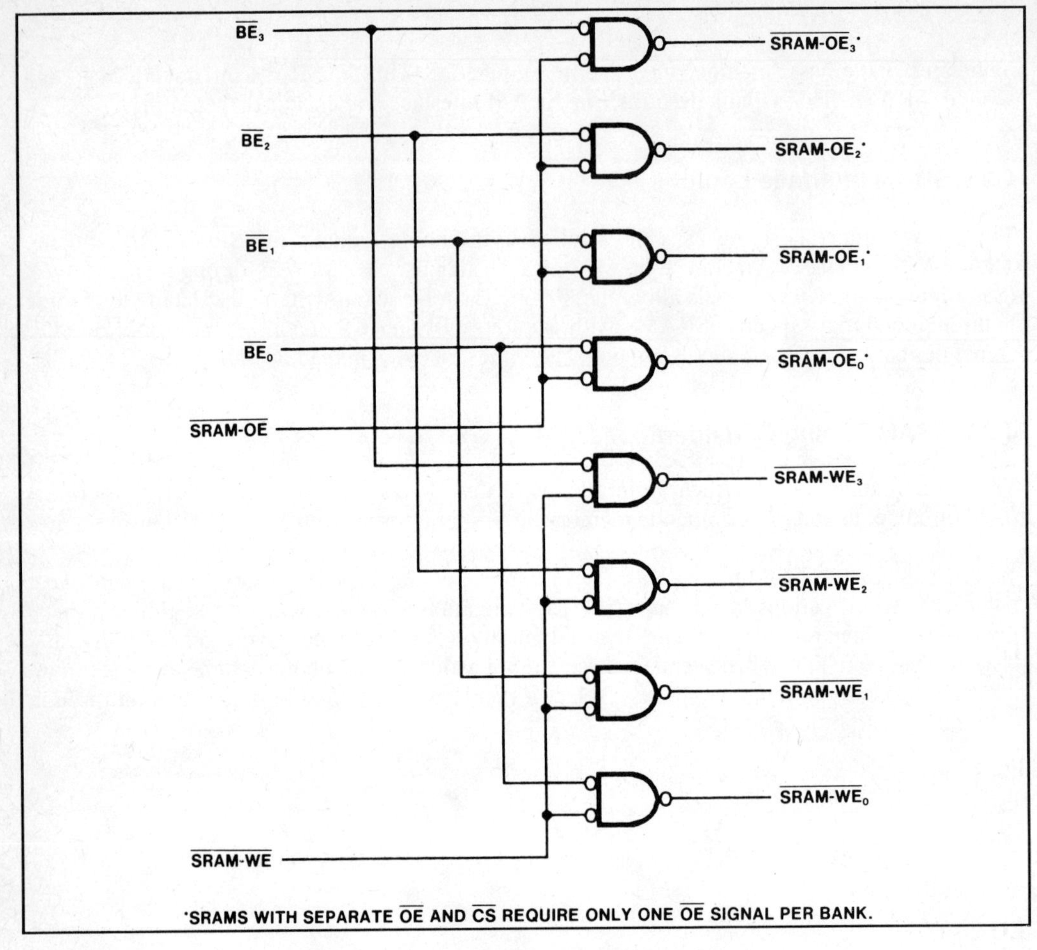

Figure 4-8: Logic Diagram for SRAM Interface

Figure 4-9 shows the critical timing path for a one-word SRAM read operation. The diagram consists of three time periods: the address setup period ($T_{addrset}$), the memory response period (T_{mem}), and the data return period ($T_{dataset}$). Note that the timing for the read command and output control signals does not enter into the critical timing path.

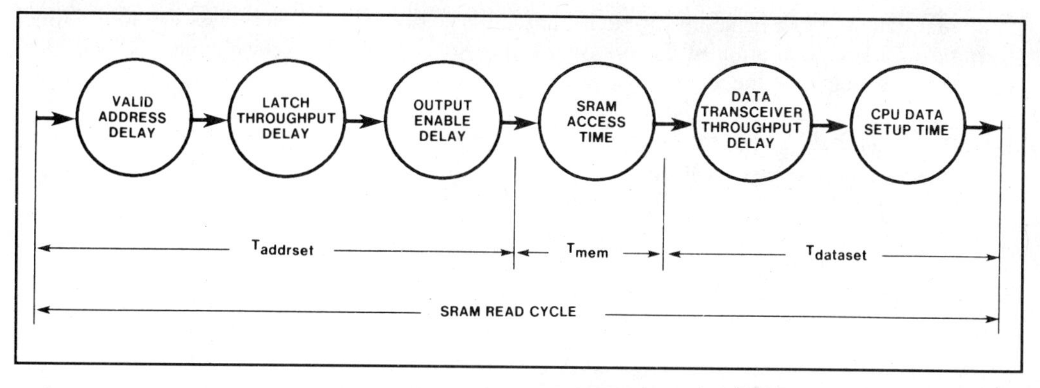

Figure 4-9: Critical Timing Path for SRAM Read Operation

During the $T_{addrset}$ period, the 80960KB processor outputs a valid address that latches on the low-to-high transition of the $\overline{\text{ALE}}$ signal. The address decoder generates the $\overline{\text{SRAM-CS}}$ signal from the latched address and the Timing Control/SRAM Interface logic subsequently generates the $\overline{\text{OE}}$ signals. During the T_{mem} period the SRAM responds to commands and signals and retrieves data. The access time of the memory determines the duration of the T_{mem} period. Delaying the $\overline{\text{READY}}$ signal causes T_{mem} to vary in increments of clock cycles.

The data must be available at the address/data pins of the processor before the end of the data state. The $T_{dataset}$ period must account for the setup time requirement of the 80960KB processor and the throughput delay of a data transceiver.

For a no-wait state operation, the data word transfer must complete in two system clock (CLK) cycles. Equation 1 can be used to determine the minimum time period for a no-wait state operation ($T_{mem\text{-}no\text{-}wait}$), where:

EQUATION 1

$$T_{mem\text{-}no\text{-}wait} = 2CLK - T_{addrset} - T_{dataset}$$

where: $T_{mem\text{-}no\text{-}wait}$ = Memory access time for no-wait state operation

2CLK = Two system clock (CLK) cycles

$T_{addrset}$ = Maximum delay to valid address
+ Maximum throughput delay of address latch
+ Maximum delay to generate chip select
+ Maximum delay to generate $\overline{\text{SRAM-OE}}$

$T_{dataset}$ = Maximum delay through data transceiver
+ Maximum data setup time of CPU

A similar equation can be setup for burst transactions. Equation 1 determines the access time for a no-wait state operation of the first word. For subsequent words, use equation 2. In this equation, the delay in the burst logic substitutes for the address setup time to change the address (T_{burst}). In this case, the data transfer of each subsequent word must complete in one system clock (CLK) cycle (no address state). The lesser value of equation 1 or equation 2 determines the minimum access time for a no-wait state operation ($T_{mem\text{-}no\text{-}wait}$).

EQUATION 2

$T_{mem\text{-}no\text{-}wait}$	$= CLK - T_{burst} - T_{dataset}$
where: $T_{mem\text{-}no\text{-}wait}$	= Memory access time for no-wait state operation
CLK	= One system clock (CLK) cycles
T_{burst}	= Maximum delay to change the address
$T_{dataset}$	= Maximum delay through data transceiver
	+ Maximum data setup time of CPU

You can delay the $\overline{READY}$ signal and add wait states to extend the memory access time.

Figure 4-10 shows the critical timing path for an SRAM write operation. The diagram consists of two time periods: the address setup period ($T_{addrset}$) and the memory response period (T_{mem}).

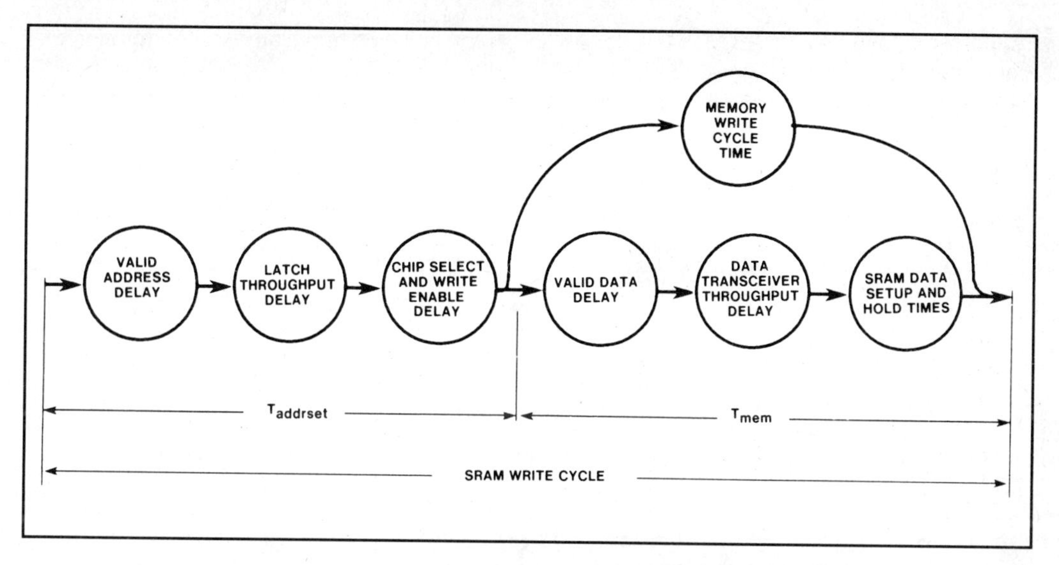

Figure 4-10: Critical Timing Path for SRAM Write Transaction

During the $T_{addrset}$ period, the 80960KB processor outputs a valid address that latches on the low-to-high transition of $\overline{ALE}$. The address decoder generates the $\overline{SRAM\text{-}CS}$ signal from the latched address.

During the T_{mem} period, the SRAM responds to the commands and writes data. The access time of the memory determines the duration of the T_{mem} period. Delaying the $\overline{READY}$ signal can vary T_{mem} in increments of clock cycles.

You should consider two timing paths during the T_{mem} period: the path where data enters memory, and the path that monitors the memory write cycle time. The first path accounts for the time when the 80960KB processor generates valid data, the time for throughput delay of a data transceiver, and the data setup time requirement of the memory. The second path is the memory write cycle specification. The longer of the two paths is the critical timing path.

4.3 DRAM CONTROLLER

This section provides design guidelines for a DRAM controller. Some DRAMs offer static column mode and $\overline{CAS}$ before $\overline{RAS}$ refresh. This section provides guidelines on how to use these features with the burst capability of the 80960KB processor to significantly enhance system throughput.

The DRAM controller multiplexes the address into a row and column address, performs the refresh operation, arbitrates between a refresh and memory requests, and generates the necessary control signals for the DRAM. To implement these functions, the memory controller uses an address multiplexer, an arbiter, a refresh interval timer, and DRAM timing and control circuitry (see Figure 4-11).

You can use a standard DRAM controller (although it typically degrades system performance).

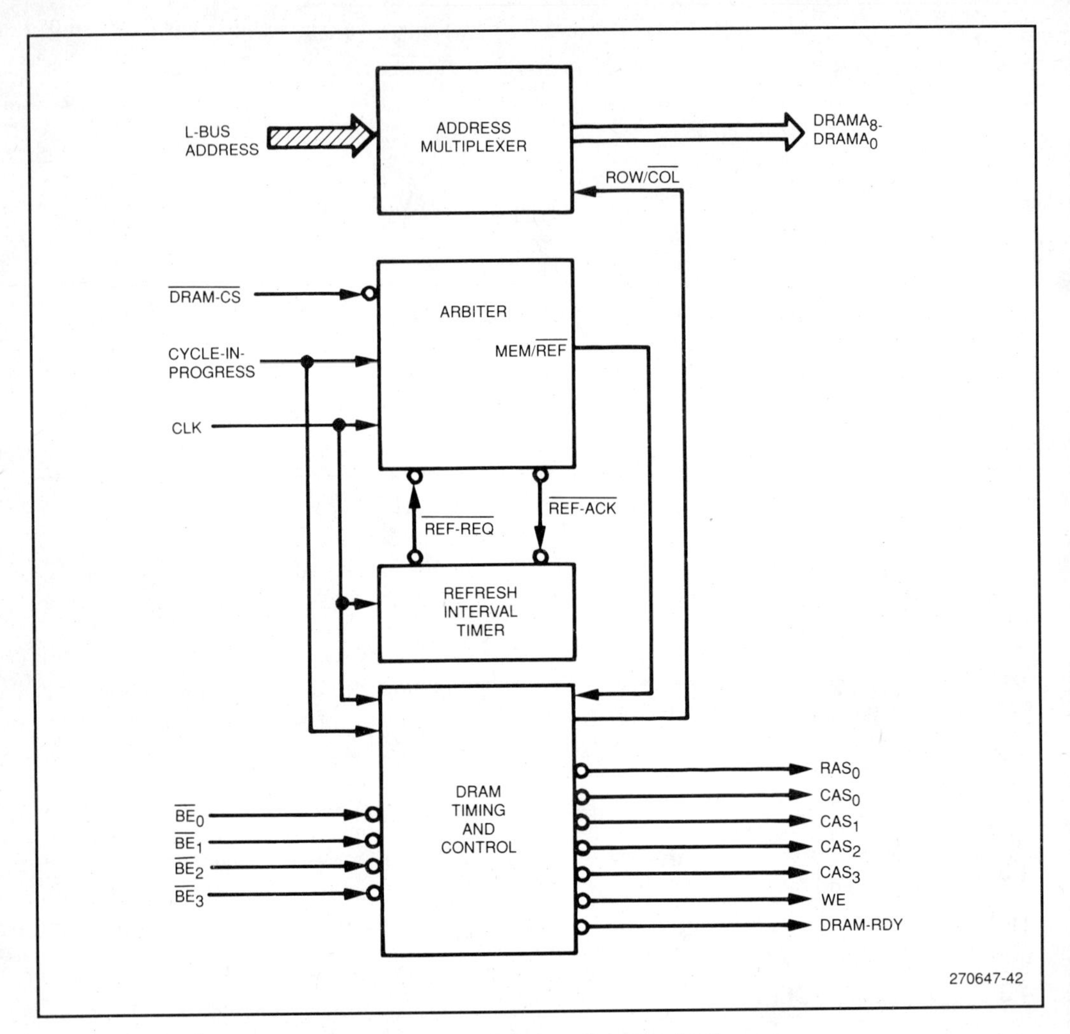

Figure 4-11: DRAM Controller Block Diagram

4.3.1 Address Multiplexer

The address multiplexer divides the DRAM address into a row and column address. The row/column select signal (ROW/$\overline{\text{COL}}$) from the DRAM timing and control circuit selects the row or column address.

4.3.2 Refresh Interval Timer

The refresh interval timer periodically generates a refresh request (REF-REQ) after counting enough bus cycles to equal the refresh interval period. Since a refresh request occurs after a completed operation, the refresh period must account for the time required to perform a bus operation (as well as the DRAM refresh specification). For example, a 1M-bit DRAM that requires 512 refresh cycles within 8 ms needs a refresh cycle every 15.6 microseconds. To meet the DRAM specification, the refresh interval timer must generate a refresh request in less than 15.6 microseconds to compensate for any time required to complete the operation with wait states.

After receiving the REF-REQ signal, the arbiter sends a refresh acknowledge signal REF-ACK back to the interval timer to assure that refresh occurs before generating another REF-REQ.

4.3.3 Arbiter

The DRAM controller uses an arbiter to decide whether the circuitry needs to perform a memory cycle or a refresh cycle. In a synchronous design, the arbiter easily performs arbitration because memory and refresh cycle requests never occur at or near the same time.

The arbiter monitors memory cycle requests and refresh requests. The arbiter decodes two signals to detect a DRAM memory request: DRAM-CS and CYCLE-IN-PROGRESS. The REF-REQ signal indicates that the arbiter must perform a refresh cycle. The arbiter arbitrates between a memory cycle or refresh cycle and generates a Memory/Refresh (MEM/REF) signal. The DRAM timing and control block uses the MEM/REF signal to start the generation of the control signals.

During a refresh cycle, the arbiter sends a REF-ACK signal to the refresh timer, which uses this signal to begin another count.

4.3.4 DRAM Timing and Control

The DRAM timing and control circuit is the final logic block and core of the DRAM controller. The functions of this circuit include the following:

- Generating the DRAM control signals (RAS, CAS, and WE) with the proper timing relationships during system operation.
- Generating the DRAM-RDY signal.
- Asserting CAS before RAS to perform the refresh function.
- Performing several DRAM-required warm-up cycles when first applying power.

The DRAM timing and control logic can take advantage of the burst-transfer capability of the 80960KB processor. The processor accomplishes this using the static column mode or nibble mode. With nibble mode, the DRAM receives a multiplexed address, and quickly transfers up to four bits of data with successive toggling of the CAS pulse. The DRAM timing and control logic can provide the successive CAS pulses using the CYCLE-IN-PROGRESS and DRAM-RDY signals. The static column mode can also take advantage of the burst capability of the DRAM. Static column mode allows fast-access to the bits within the selected row of the DRAM. It changes the column address after the first access to accomplish this.

Figure 4-12 shows a flow chart for the DRAM timing and control logic using static column mode. The DRAM timing and control circuit receives a refresh request or a memory request on the MEM/$\overline{\text{REF}}$ and CYCLE-IN-PROGRESS input signals. For a memory request, DRAM timing and control determines whether it needs a read or a write operation from the W/$\overline{\text{R}}$ pin on the 80960KB processor.

For a read operation, the DRAM timing and control logic performs similar functions on the first word: it asserts $\overline{\text{WE}}$; it brings ROW/$\overline{\text{COL}}$ high to select a row address; it asserts $\overline{\text{RAS}_0}$; it brings ROW/$\overline{\text{COL}}$ low to select the column address; it asserts $\overline{\text{CAS}_3}$ through $\overline{\text{CAS}_0}$ (derived from the four latched byte enable signals); and it generates a $\overline{\text{DRAM-RDY}}$ signal. The $\overline{\text{DRAM-RDY}}$ signal causes the burst logic to increment the address and informs the 80960KB processor that the data word was written.

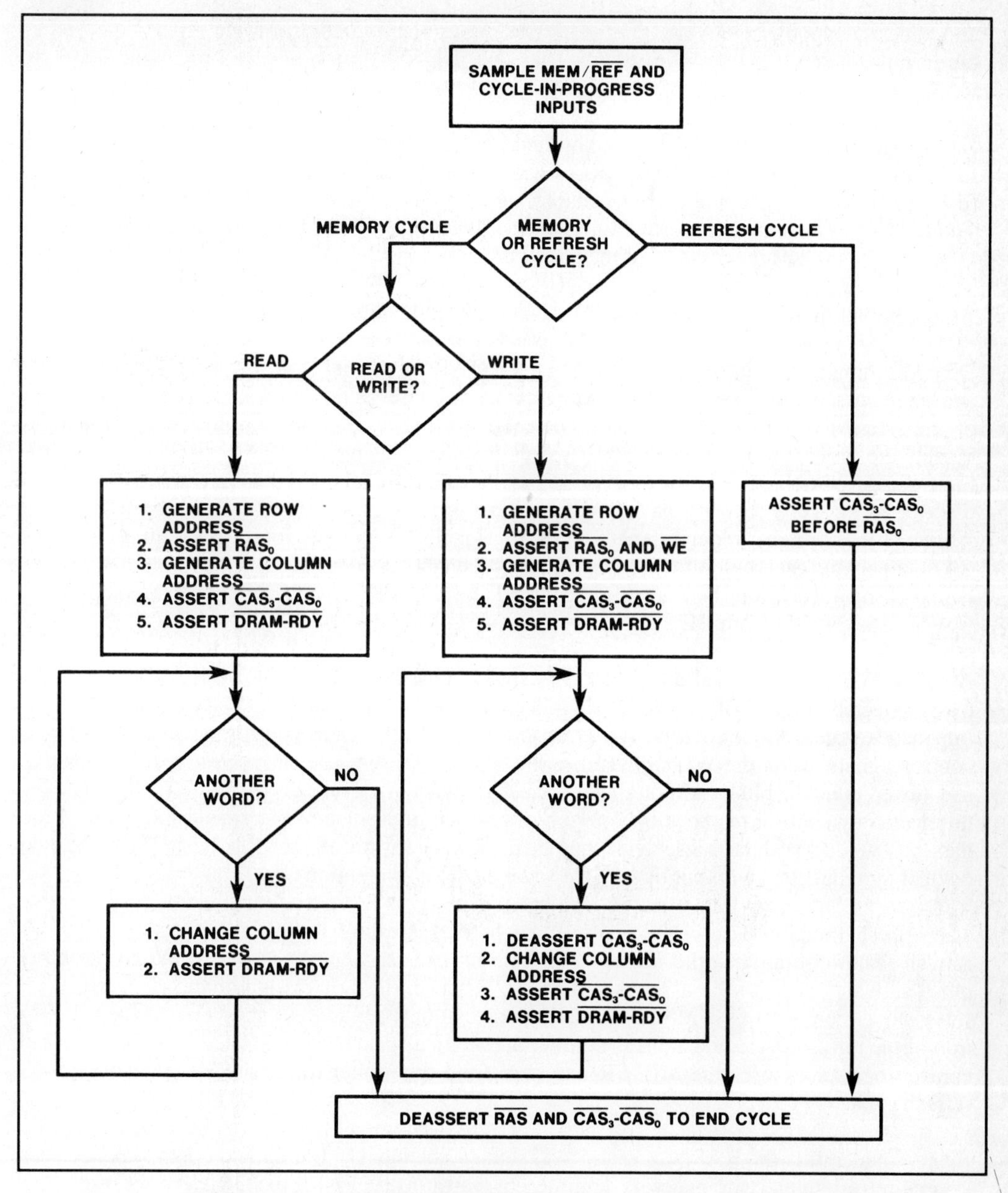

Figure 4-12: Flow Chart for DRAM Timing and Control Logic

After completing these functions, the DRAM timing and control logic samples the CYCLE-IN-PROGRESS to determine whether to transfer another data word. If so, the DRAM timing and control logic maintains the ROW/$\overline{COL}$ signal low to select the new column address, deasserts and asserts $\overline{CAS_3}$ through $\overline{CAS_0}$ to observe the CAS precharge specification of the DRAM, and generates another $\overline{\text{DRAM-RDY}}$. The DRAM timing and control logic repeats the procedure until all the data words transfer. Then, the DRAM timing and control logic deasserts $\overline{\text{RAS}}_0$.

For a write operation, the DRAM timing and control logic performs similar functions on the first word: it asserts $\overline{\text{WE}}$; it brings ROW/$\overline{\text{COL}}$ high to select a row address; it asserts $\overline{\text{RAS}}_0$ (derived from the four latched byte enable signals); and it generates a $\overline{\text{DRAM-RDY}}$ signal. The $\overline{\text{DRAM-RDY}}$ signal causes the burst logic to increment the address and asserts $\overline{\text{READY}}$ to inform the 80960KB processor that the data word was written.

After completing these functions, the DRAM timing and control logic samples the CYCLE-IN-PROGRESS to determine whether the 80960KB needs to transfer another data word. If so, the DRAM timing and control logic maintains the ROW/$\overline{\text{COL}}$ signal low to select the new column address, deasserts and asserts $\overline{\text{CAS}}_3$ through $\overline{\text{CAS}}_0$ to observe the CAS precharge specification of the DRAM and generates another $\overline{\text{DRAM-RDY}}$. The DRAM timing and control logic repeats the procedure until all the data words transfer. Then, the DRAM timing and control logic deasserts $\overline{\text{RAS}}_0$.

Although the circuitry requires only one $\overline{\text{RAS}}$ signal, it generates four $\overline{\text{CAS}}$ signals ($\overline{\text{CAS}}_3$ - $\overline{\text{CAS}}_0$) to enable each byte of the L-bus. The byte enable decoder generates these $\overline{\text{CAS}}$ signals, which correspond to the byte enable signals of the 80960KB processor. For example, $\overline{\text{CAS}}_0$, which maps directly from $\overline{\text{BE}}_0$, selects the least significant data byte ($\overline{\text{LAD}}_7$ - $\overline{\text{LAD}}_0$).

A single $\overline{\text{WE}}$ control signal and four $\overline{\text{CAS}}$ signals ensure the enabling of only those DRAM bytes selected for a write cycle. All other data bytes maintain their outputs in the high-impedance state. A common design error is to use a single $\overline{\text{CAS}}$ control signal and four $\overline{\text{WE}}$ control signals, using the $\overline{\text{WE}}$ signals to write the DRAM bytes selectively in write cycles that use fewer than 32 bits. Although the selected bytes write correctly, the circuitry enables unselected bytes for a read cycle. These bytes present their data to the unselected bytes of the data bus while the data transceivers output data to every bit of the data bus. When the two devices simultaneously output data to the same bus, bus contention occurs.

The refresh function asserts the $\overline{\text{CAS}}$ signal before asserting $\overline{\text{RAS}}$. The $\overline{\text{CAS}}$ before $\overline{\text{RAS}}$ refresh feature eliminates the need for an external refresh address counter. When the $\overline{\text{CAS}}$ pulse activates prior to the assertion of the $\overline{\text{RAS}}$ pulse, the DRAM automatically performs a refresh cycle on one row with the employment of an on-chip address counter. At the completion of the refresh cycle, the address counter automatically increments. The DRAM timing and control logic block uses the MEM/$\overline{\text{REF}}$ signal from the arbiter to initiate a $\overline{\text{CAS}}$ before $\overline{\text{RAS}}$ refresh cycle.

Besides generating the $\overline{\text{RAS}}$, $\overline{\text{CAS}}$, and $\overline{\text{WE}}$ signals, the DRAM timing and control logic issues several refresh requests to generate a number of warm-up cycles for the DRAM after reset.

4.3.5 Timing Considerations for the DRAM Controller

Figure 4-13 shows a typical example of a timing diagram for a two-word read transaction that uses static column mode; similarly, Figure 4-14 illustrates a typical example for a two-word write transaction. The example assumes a memory access time that requires two wait states (T_w) for the initial data word and one wait for the second data word.

Circled numbers in the diagrams below note critical timing areas for both read and write transactions.

1. The delay for the CPU to generate a valid address.
2. The delay for the DRAM timing and control logic to generate the CYCLE-IN-PROGRESS signal.
3. The delay to generate the DRAM row address. This interval includes the address latch throughput delay, the multiplexer throughput delay, and the address driver delay.
4. The delay to generate $\overline{\text{RAS}}$, which includes the delay to generate the $\overline{\text{DRAM-CS}}$ signal.
5. The row address hold time after the high-to-low transition of $\overline{\text{RAS}}$.
6. The time required to generate the multiplexer control signal (ROW/$\overline{\text{COL}}$) after satisfying the row address hold time.
7. The time required to switch from a row to column address plus any driver delays.
8. The delay to generate and drive the $\overline{\text{CAS}}$ signals.
9. For a read transaction, the throughput delay of the data transceivers. For a write transaction, the CPU delay to generate valid data.
10. For a read transaction, the data setup time of the CPU. For a write transaction, the throughput delay of the data transceivers.
11. The time required to increment and drive the column address.
12. For a write transaction only, the delay time to bring $\overline{\text{CAS}}$ high (terminate the $\overline{\text{CAS}}$ pulse for the first data byte), to precharge the $\overline{\text{CAS}}$ pulse (that the DRAM requires), and to assert $\overline{\text{CAS}}$ again.
13. The $\overline{\text{RAS}}$ precharge time, which must occur before another memory cycle begins.

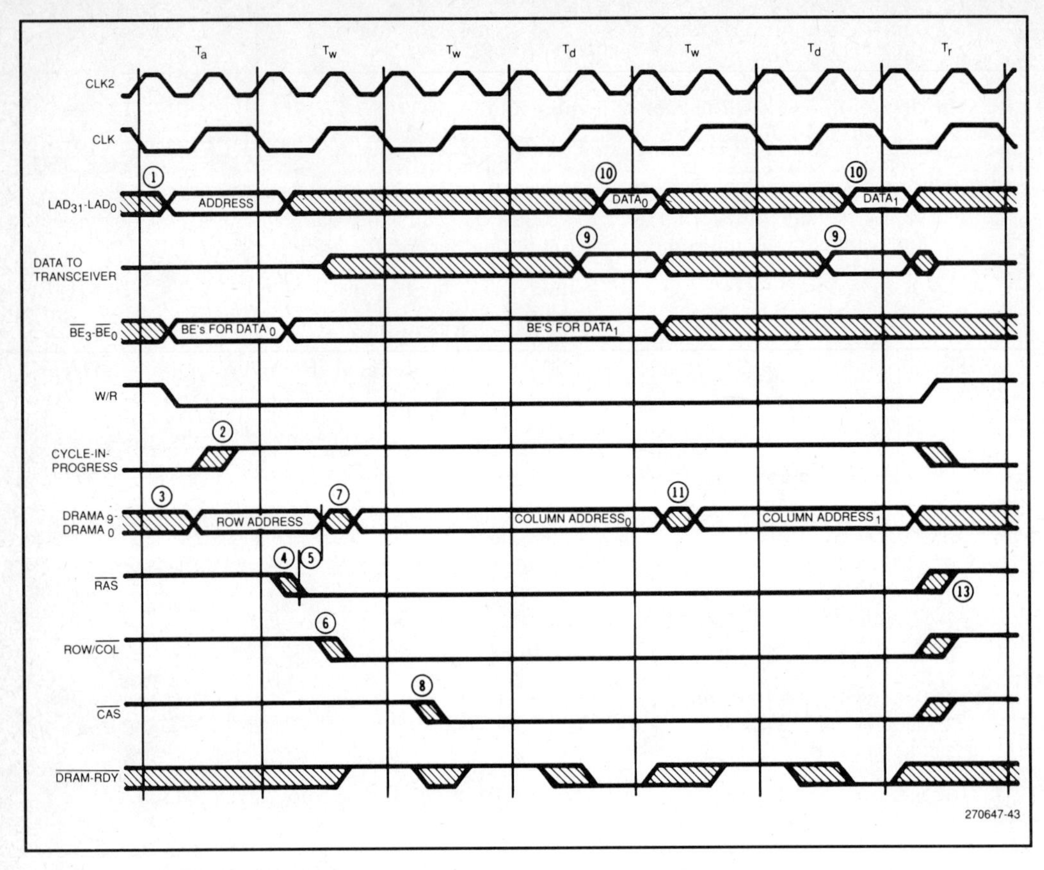

Figure 4-13: Timing Diagram for Two-word DRAM Read Transaction

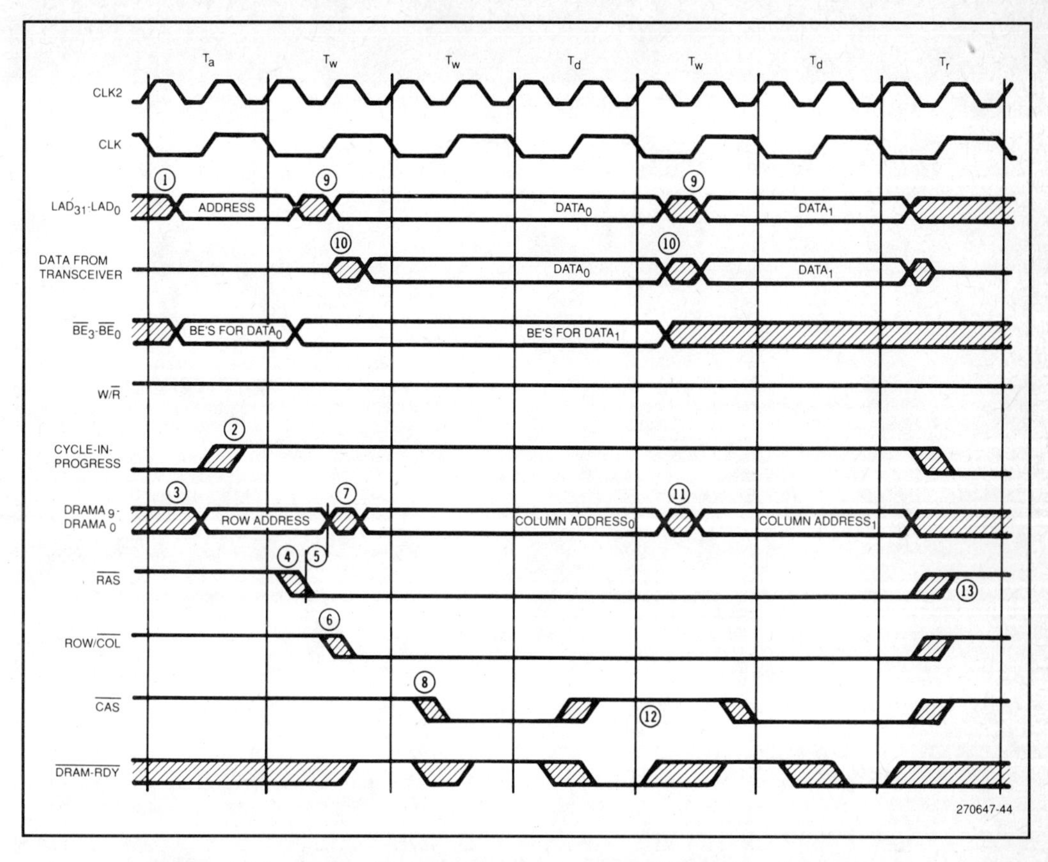

Figure 4-14: Timing Diagram for Two-word DRAM Write Transaction

4.4 SUMMARY

The memory interface circuit allows the 80960KB processor to communicate with the memory devices. The basic memory interface logic divides into six blocks: the data transceivers, the address latches, the address decoder, the burst logic, the DRAM timing and control logic, and the byte enable latch. The DRAM controller and SRAM interface complete the memory interface circuit. The DRAM controller can take advantage of the 80960KB processor's burst capability to enhance system performance.

I/O Interface 5

CHAPTER 5
I/O INTERFACE

The 80960KB processor maps 8-, 16-, and 32-bit I/O devices into a 4-Gbyte memory address space. This chapter describes the design considerations for the interface between the 80960KB processor and its associated I/O components. Several examples illustrate the design concepts.

5.1 INTERFACING TO 8-BIT AND 16-BIT PERIPHERALS

The 80960KB processor uses a memory-mapped address to access I/O devices. Consequently, memory-type instructions can perform input/output (I/O) operations. For example, the 80960KB processor's LOAD and STORE instructions can directly support 8-bit and 16-bit data moves to or from I/O peripherals. The instructions include those listed below.

- Load Ordinal Byte (reads a byte)
- Load Ordinal Short (reads 16-bit data)
- Store Ordinal Byte (writes a byte)
- Store Ordinal Short (writes 16-bit data)

These instructions specify the two low-order lines of the effective address to perform a transfer operation on the data bits. See the *80960KB CPU Programmer's Reference Manual* for complete details.

5.2 GENERAL SYSTEM INTERFACE

In a typical 80960KB processor system design, a general system interface controls a number of slave I/O devices. Other I/O devices, particularly those capable of controlling the L-bus, can use the general system interface, but may require additional logic to isolate the bus. This section describes the general system interface and assumes that the 80960KB processor does not perform burst transactions to the I/O devices.

Figure 5-1 shows the major logic blocks of the general system interface. Standard 8-bit data transceivers add drive capability, provide bus isolation, and prevent bus conflicts that may occur with slow I/O components. The address latch demultiplexes the address/data lines and holds the address stable throughout the L-bus transaction. The address decoder generates the I/O chip-select signals from the latched address lines. The timing control block provides the $\overline{\text{READY}}$ signal and the I/O read and I/O write command to the 80960KB processor.

This basic interface circuit is quite similar to the basic memory interface described in Chapter 4. For most systems, the same data transceivers, address decoders, and address latches can access both memory and I/O devices; the timing control logic can accommodate both memory and I/O devices.

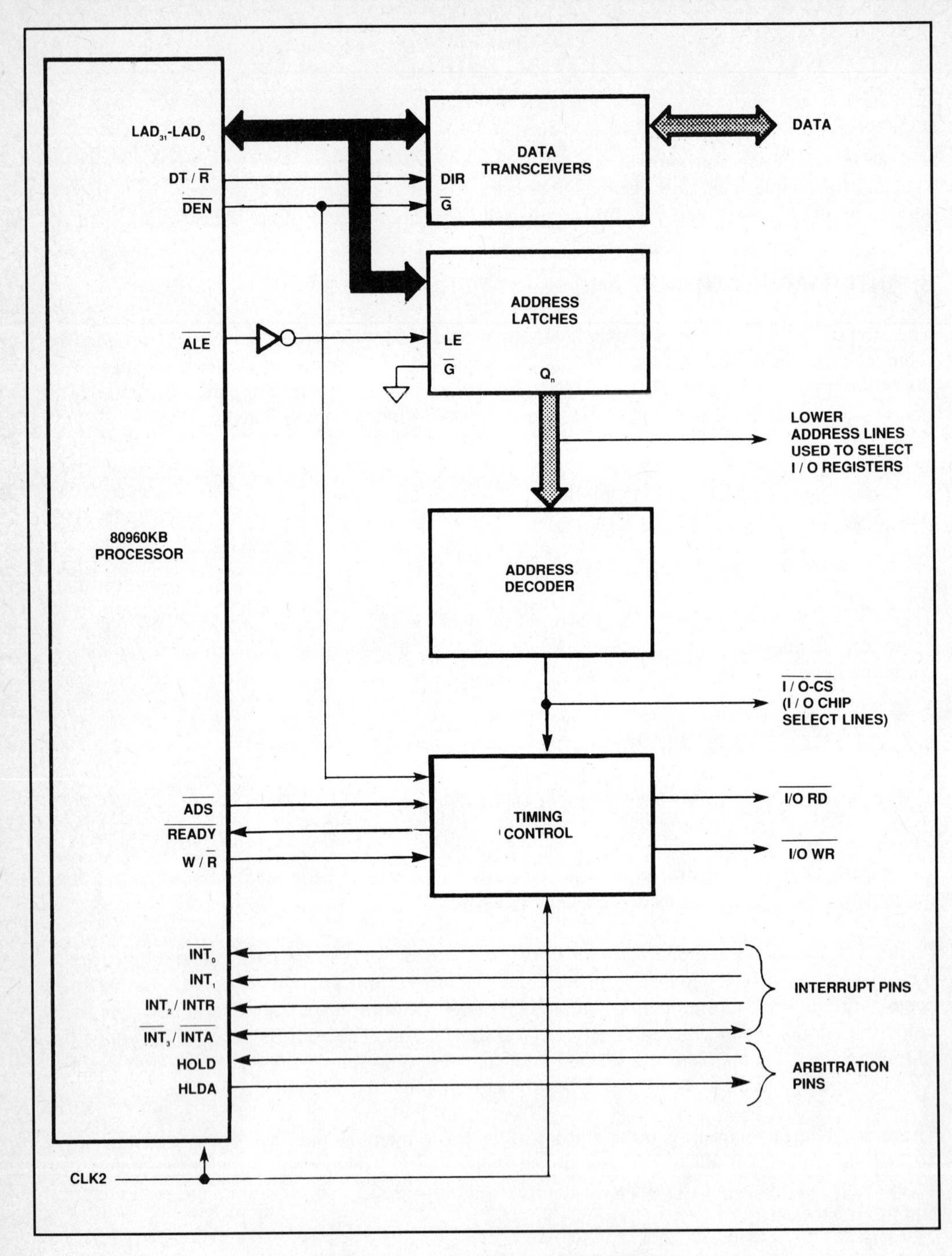

Figure 5-1: Simplified I/O Interface

5.2.1 Data Transceivers

Standard 8-bit transceivers can provide isolation and additional drive capability for the L-bus. Transceivers prevent bus contention that can occur if some devices are slow to remove data from the data bus after a read cycle. For example, if an I/O write cycle follows an I/O read cycle, the 80960KB processor may drive the L-bus before a slow device removes its outputs from the bus. This could potentially cause a current spike. You can omit transceivers, however, if the data float time of the device is short enough and the load does not exceed the 80960KB device specifications.

Two signals from the 80960KB processor, Data Transmit/Receive ($DT/\overline{R}$) and Data Enable ($\overline{DEN}$) can control the data transceiver. The signal $DT/\overline{R}$ indicates the direction of data flow, while $\overline{DEN}$ enables the transceivers.

5.2.2 Address Latch/Demultiplexer

Standard transparent latches can demultiplex the address/data lines of the 80960KB processor. The $\overline{ALE}$ signal from the 80960KB processor controls the $\overline{ALE}$ latch. The $\overline{ALE}$ signal passes through an inverter, such that when $\overline{ALE}$ goes low, the address flows through the latch. The low-to-high transition of $\overline{ALE}$ can latch the address.

If a system only uses slave type peripherals, the output enable signal of the latches can remain active if it connects to ground. For systems with DMA devices, the output enable signal can permit the DMA device to drive a common address bus.

5.2.3 Address Decoder

The address decoder determines which particular I/O device the processor selects when it decodes the address. The I/O address may be any address in the 4-Gbyte address range except for the upper 16Mbytes (addresses $FF000000_{16}$ through $FFFFFFFF_{16}$). The 80960KB processor reserves these addresses for interagent communication (IAC's) and internal I/O.

A small range of reserved address bits may be used to define certain high-order address bits as an I/O access. As an example, considering a 32-bit address, A_{31} through A_{15} would indicate an I/O access when bit A_{31} sets to zero, and bits A_{30}-A_{15} set to one. A_{14} through A_5 would then specify a particular I/O device while A_4 through A_2 would access up to 8 registers of the I/O component. The I/O device does not use bits A_1 and A. This particular scheme selects up to 1,024 devices, while using only 32-Kbytes of the available 4-Gbytes of address space.

You can place the address decoder either before or after the address latches. Usually, it is placed after the latches so that the chip-select signal does not need an additional latch.

5.2.4 Timing Control Logic

The timing control logic inserts Wait States to accommodate I/O devices that cannot transfer information until data becomes available. The timing control logic consists of a counter and timing logic (see Figure 5-2).The counter produces a 4-bit binary count. The count begins with the operation determined by $\overline{ADS}$ and $\overline{DEN}$, and ends with the $\overline{READY}$ signal. Based upon the clock count, the I/O chip select signal ($\overline{I/O\text{-}CS0}$, and the W/$\overline{R}$ command, the timing logic asserts the $\overline{READY}$ signal, the I/O write command ($\overline{I/O\text{-}WR}$), and the I/O read command ($\overline{I/O\text{-}RD}$).

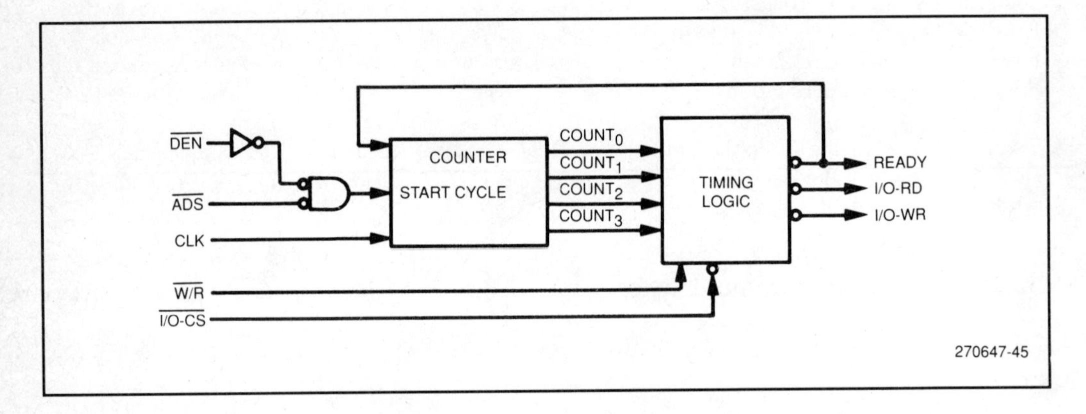

Figure 5-2: I/O Timing Control Block Diagram

For many peripherals, you can program the timing logic to assert $\overline{READY}$ at the appropriate count for the selected device. Specific I/O chip select signals can indicate how many clock cycles to wait before asserting $\overline{READY}$.

For some I/O peripherals, particularly bus masters, counting clock cycles cannot determine the $\overline{READY}$ signal. For these I/O devices, the device must supply the $\overline{READY}$ signal and pass it on to the 80960KB processor.

The timing control block can assert the $\overline{I/O\text{-}RD}$ or $\overline{I/O\text{-}WR}$ signals for I/O devices based upon the clock count. You can select timing for these signals to accommodate the slowest device. This simplifies the logic circuit or customizes each individual peripheral device to maximize performance.

5.3 I/O INTERFACE DESIGN EXAMPLES

The general system interface shown in Figure 5-1 connects the 80960KB processor to many slave peripherals. The following list includes some common peripherals compatible with this interface:

- 8259A Programmable Interrupt Controller
- 8253, 8254 Programmable Interval Timer
- 82510, Asynchronous Serial Controller
- 8274, 82530 Multi-Protocol Serial Controller
- 8255 Programmable Peripheral Interface

- 82586 LAN Co-processor (not offered in a MILSTD883C version)
- 82786 Graphics Co-processor

This section provides guidelines and design considerations for interfacing the 80960KB processor to different types of I/O configurations. Specifically, this section examines several design examples. The 8259A design example shows how to interface the 80960KB processor to a slave-type peripheral device. The 82586 design example shows how a 16-bit bus master reads and writes to the 80960KB processor's system memory. The 82786 design example shows how the 80960KB processor can read or write to graphic memory using a 16-bit data bus.

5.3.1 8259A Programmable Interrupt Controller

You can use the 8259A Programmable Interrupt Controller for interrupt-driven microcomputer systems, where it manages up to eight independent interrupts. The 8259A handles interrupt-priority resolution and returns an 8-bit vector to the 80960KB processor during an interrupt acknowledge cycle. The Intel and Application Note AP-59 contains detailed information for 8259A configurations.

5.3.2 Interface

Figure 5-3 shows the connection of the 80960KB processor to a single 8259A Interrupt Controller. This circuit consists of the general system interface plus a bi-directional buffer. The example assumes that several interrupt requests occur at the same time, requiring a priority resolution.

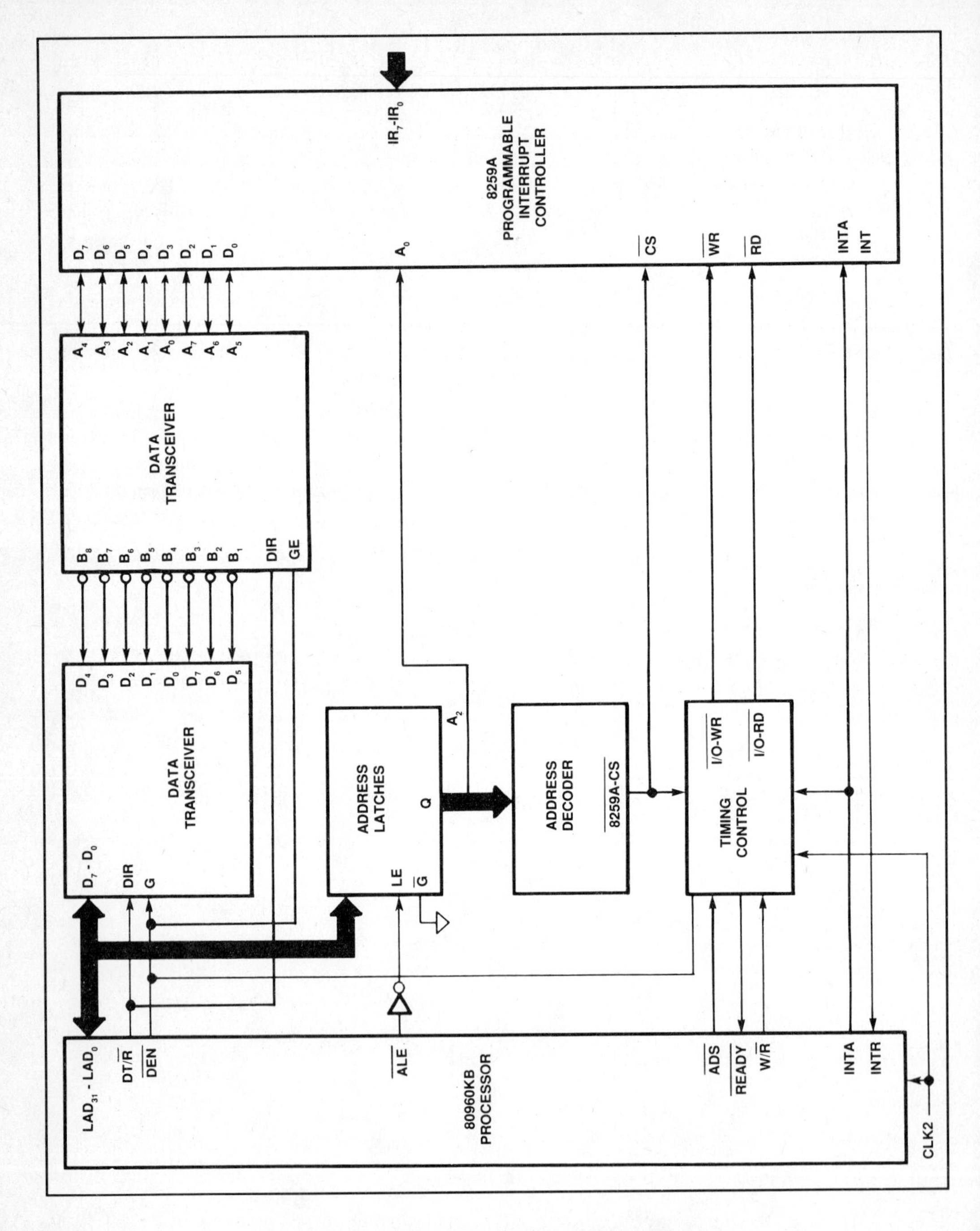

Figure 5-3: Block Diagram for 8259A Interface

The data lines from the 8259A do not directly align with the 80960KB processor because of the difference in priority resolution between the devices. Although both devices use an 8-bit interrupt vector, the 80960KB processor implicitly defines the priority. The 8259A divides the interrupt vector by eight to define the priority in the lower three bits of the interrupt vector. Furthermore, the highest priority vector of the 80960KB processor has a value of 31 in the upper five bits of the interrupt vector. Whereas, the highest priority interrupt of the 8259A has a value of 0 in the lower three bits of the interrupt vector.

To resolve the priority difference, the programmer/designer should invert and rotate the interrupt vector left three bits from the 8259A (see Figure 5-3). Care must be exercised, however, when programming the 8259A. For example, assuming that the second initialization command word (ICW2 register) of the 8259A requires a data byte value of 00011111_2. To transfer the correct information, the 80960KB processor needs to write a data word with the value of 00000111_2 because this word is inverted and rotated left three places.

5.3.3 Operation

The 8259A begins the interrupt cycle when it generates an interrupt request (INT) to the 80960KB processor, which receives the signal on its INTR input pin (this assumes the Interrupt Control Register of the 80960KB processor is set to accommodate an external interrupt controller).

When the 80960KB processor comes to a breakpoint in its execution, it asserts the $\overline{\text{INTA}}$ signal twice. The first $\overline{\text{INTA}}$ signal acknowledges the interrupt request and causes the 8259A to assign priorities to the interrupt requests it receives up to that point. The processor applies $\overline{\text{INTA}}$ to the timing control logic to generate the $\overline{\text{READY}}$ signal.

The 80960KB processor automatically asserts the second $\overline{\text{INTA}}$ signal five clock cycles after the assertion of $\overline{\text{READY}}$. After the second assertion of $\overline{\text{INTA}}$, the 80960KB processor reads the interrupt vector from the 8259A.

The bidirectional buffer inverts and passes the 8-bit vector to the 80960KB processor with the appropriate lines rearranged. The signal $\overline{\text{INTA}}$ controls the output enable signal for the data buffer for this operation. After the data transfer is complete, the timing control circuit generates a second $\overline{\text{READY}}$ signal to terminate the interrupt acknowledge cycle.

The same circuitry can read or write to the 8259A registers. In this case, the 80960KB processor selects the 8259A through a memory-mapped address. Local address line 2 (A2) selects one of two internal registers of the 8259A. The timing control circuit generates the I/O read or I/O write command. The data passes through the data transceiver to or from the selected register of the 8259A.

5.3.4 82530 Serial Communication Controller

The 82530 Serial Communication Controller is a dual-channel, multi-protocol controller with on-chip baud rate generators, digital phase locked loops, various data encode/decode circuits, and extensive diagnostic capabilities. The 82530 interfaces with high-speed serial communications lines using a variety of communication protocols, including asynchronous, synchronous, and HDLC/SDLC protocols. The 82530 contains two independent full-duplex channels.

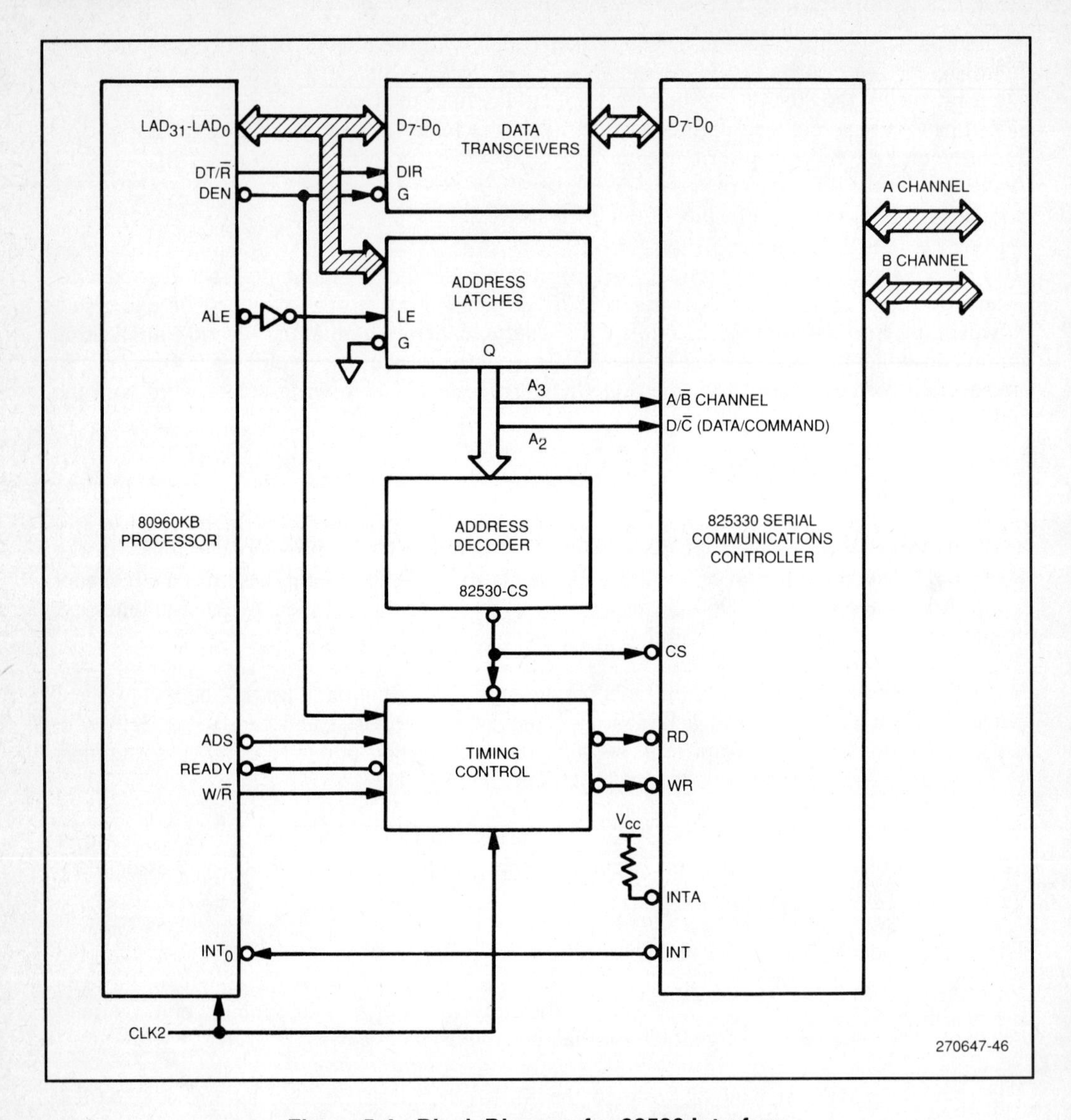

Figure 5-4: Block Diagram for 82530 Interface

The general system interface circuit can connect the 80960KB processor to the 82530 (see Figure 5-4). The 82530 sends an interrupt request to the 80960KB processor as shown or it sends the interrupt request to an interrupt controller, which in turn sends it to the 80960KB processor. The 80960KB processor responds to the interrupt request and issues an address.

After the component latches the address, the processor decodes the address lines to generate a chip-select signal, which activates the 82530.

The lower two address lines, A2 and A3, select the channel and command/data. A2 connects to the Channel-A/Channel-B select input pin. This selects the channel that performs the serial read or write operations. A3 connects to the Data/Command ($D/\overline{C}$) select input pin. This signal defines the type of information that transfers to or from the 82530 on the data lines (D7 through D0). A high level means that data transfers; a low level indicates a command.

The timing control circuit generates an I/O read or I/O write command based upon the $W/\overline{R}$ command from the 80960KB processor. When the data transfer completes, the timing control circuit sends a signal to terminate the transaction. The programmer can select baud rate clocks in several ways, including the use of an external crystal.

5.3.5 82586 Local Area Network Co-processor Example

The 82586 is an intelligent, high-performance communications controller which performs most tasks required for controlling access to a local area network (LAN), such as Ethernet or Starlan. In many applications, the 82586 is the communication manager for a station that connects to a LAN controller. Such a station usually includes a host CPU, shared memory, a Serial Interface Unit, a transceiver, and a LAN controller link. The 82586 performs all functions associated with data transfer between the shared memory and the LAN link, including:

- Framing
- Link management
- Address filtering
- Error detection
- Data encoding
- Network management
- Direct memory access
- Buffer chaining
- High-level (user) command interpretation

The 82586 has two interfaces: a 16-bit bus interface and a network interface to the Serial Interface Unit. This section describes the bus interface. For detailed information about the use of the 82586, refer to the *Local Area Networking Component User's Manual.*

5.3.6 Interface

There are several ways to design an interface between the 82586 and the 80960KB processor. The chosen design example shows how to interface the 82586 using a shared bus. In this example, the 82586 operates in minimum mode at one-half the processor clock frequency.

The primary function of the interface circuit is to allow the 82586 to read and write 16-bit data using the 32-bit L-bus. You will need to add high-order address lines and translate the 16-bit data lines to the 32-bit data lines with the byte enable signals to accomplish this.

Figure 5-5 shows the 82586 interface circuit, which includes the DRAM controller (see the *DRAM Controller* section in Chapter 4). This interface uses the general system interface circuit plus other logic units that specifically pertain to the 82586; i.e., the LAN data transceivers, the byte enable converter, and the LAN address latches. Shaded boxes highlight these logic blocks.

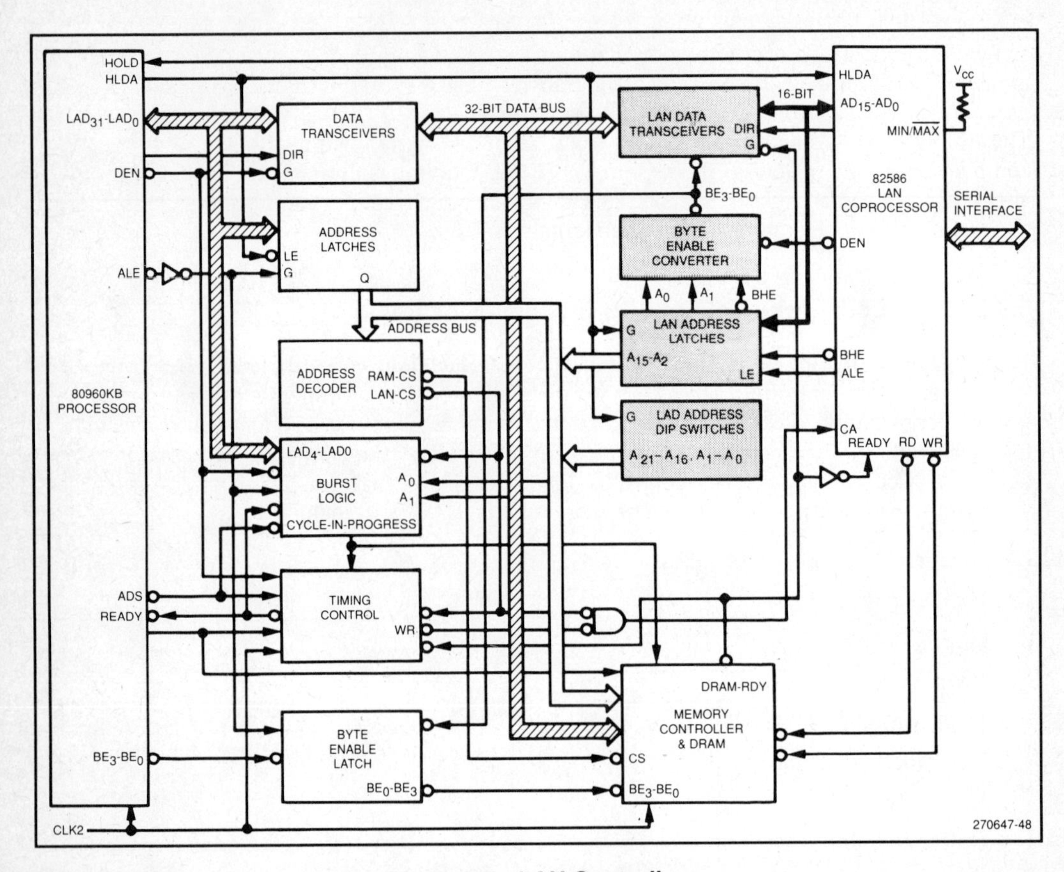

Figure 5-5: LAN Controller

The LAN data transceivers connect 16 data lines from the 82586 to both the upper and lower 16 bits of the L-bus. You convert A_0, A_1, and the $\overline{BHE}$ signal to four byte-enable signals (see Figure 5-5). The A_1 signal selects between the upper and lower 16-bit data lines; The A_0 signal selects the lower data byte for either the upper or lower 16-bit data lines. The byte-high enable signal ($\overline{BHE}$) selects the upper data byte for either the upper or lower 16-bit data lines. Date flows through the buffers when the logic asserts the appropriate byte enable signal. The DT/$\overline{R}$ signal of the 82586 controls the direction of the data flow.

The LAN address latches demultiplex AD_{15} through AD_0. The address lines and $\overline{BHE}$ latch with the $\overline{ALE}$ signal from the 82586. The hardware-programmable switches generate the

upper address lines (A_{31} through A_{16}). The 82586 begins operation with the assertion of the Channel Attention (CA) input signal. The write command and 82586 chip select signal generate this signal.

5.3.7 Operation

The interaction between the 82586 and the 80960KB processor is described below.

- The 80960KB processor supplies a memory-mapped address and a write command to invoke the 82586. The memory-mapped address results in a $\overline{\text{82586-CS}}$ signal, which gates with a write command to produce the CA signal.
- In response, the 82586 generates a hold request and waits for HLDA.
- The 80960KB processor asserts HLDA, which enables the outputs of the LAN address latches and disables the outputs of the address latches next to the 80960KB processor. The HLDA signal also gives control of the L-bus to the 82586.
- After the 82586 assumes control of the bus, it generates a 16-bit address (AD_{15} through AD_0), an $\overline{\text{ALE}}$ signal, and a $\overline{\text{BHE}}$ signal. The programmable DIP switches provide the upper address lines for the L-bus.
- Signals A_1 and A (from the 82586), and $\overline{\text{BHE}}$ decode to generate four byte enable signals ($\overline{\text{BE}}_3$ through $\overline{\text{BE}}_0$). $\overline{\text{DEN}}$ enables the output of the byte enable converter.
- DT/$\overline{\text{R}}$ from the 82586 controls the direction of the data flow through the buffers.
- The 82586 asserts the read or write signal to the DRAM controller.
- The 82586 uses the DRAM controller to access DRAM.
- The DRAM controller asserts the signal $\overline{\text{DRAM-RDY}}$. This action enables the output of the LAN data transceiver and terminates the 82586 memory cycle. The timing control logic passes the $\overline{\text{DRAM-RDY}}$ signal as the $\overline{\text{READY}}$ signal to the 82586.
- The 82586 deasserts HOLD and the 80960KB processor deasserts HLDA. The 80960KB processor regains control of bus.

5.3.8 82786 Graphics Co-processor Example

The 82786 is a high performance graphics co-processor that provides high quality text and advanced display control. It provides full support for graphics primitives at up to 25 million pixels per second and bit-mapped text up to 25 thousand characters per second. This graphics processor supports advanced features such as hardware windows, zooming, panning, and scrolling. The Intel Application Note AP-259 and Application Note AP-270 contain detailed information on the 82786.

When using the 82786, it may be necessary for the 80960KB processor to write to graphics memory. The following interface design example illustrates how the 80960KB processor can transfer a 32-bit data word to the 16-bit data bus of the 82786.

5.3.9 Interface

There are several ways to design an interface between the 82786 and the 80960KB processor. In this example, the 80960KB processor accesses the 82786 through the interface logic circuit to read or write to graphics memory. This example assumes that the 82786 operates in the slave mode, and that the 80960KB processor does not perform burst transfers. The 80960KB processor only performs burst transfers for instructions that specify accesses for more than one word or for instruction fetches.

The interface circuit divides the data lines into the upper and lower 16-bits and sequences the data transmission to translate a 32-bit data bus to a 16-bit data bus. When the 80960KB processor writes to graphics memory, the bidirectional transceivers sequence the lower and the upper data bits of the L-bus to the 16-bit data bus of the 82786.

The process reverses when the 80960KB processor reads from graphics memory. The bidirectional transceivers form a 32-bit data word. The transceivers first latch the 16-bit data word on the lower data lines, route the next 16 bits to the upper data lines, then pass the 32-bit data word on the L-bus.

Figure 5-6 shows the details of the graphics controller interface circuit. This interface uses the general system interface circuit plus the following logic units: the bidirectional transceivers, the data buffer control, the data bus controller, and the address translator. The shaded boxes highlight these logic blocks.

The bidirectional transceivers pass exchange data between a 32-bit data bus and a 16-bit data bus. Data sequences through the transceivers with the aid of control signals from the data buffer controller.

The data buffer control logic generates the signals that operate and sequence the bidirectional transceivers. The direction signal for data flow through the transceivers derives from the W/$\overline{\text{R}}$ signal of the 80960KB processor. The data buffer control logic generates four output enable signals: $\overline{\text{GAB}}_L$ enables the outputs on the B side for the lower 16 bits; $\overline{\text{GBA}}_L$ enables the outputs on the A side for the lower 16 bits; $\overline{\text{GAB}}_H$ enables the outputs on the B side for the higher 16 bits; and $\overline{\text{GBA}}_H$ enables the outputs on the A side for the higher 16 bits. The byte enable signals produce these output enable signals. The 82786 activates the slave enable signal (SEN) to assist in the assertion of the output enable signals.

The select lines for the bidirectional transceivers allow data to flow from either the latched data or the input pins. These lines (not shown) can be hardwired.

The data bus controller provides the read (RD) and write (WR) commands, memory or I/O signal (M/$\overline{\text{IO}}$), and a $\overline{\text{READY}}$ signal. This circuit generates two read or write commands for every 32-bit data transfer to or from the 80960KB processor (one for each 16-bit data transfer). The data bus controller starts counting clock cycles with the assertion of signals $\overline{\text{82786-CS}}$ and CYCLE-IN-PROGRESS. At the proper time (based upon clock counts), the controller asserts the read/write command. The controller produces $\overline{\text{READY}}$ after receiving the SEN signal from the 82786. The $\overline{\text{READY}}$ signal resets the count, and generates another read/write command.

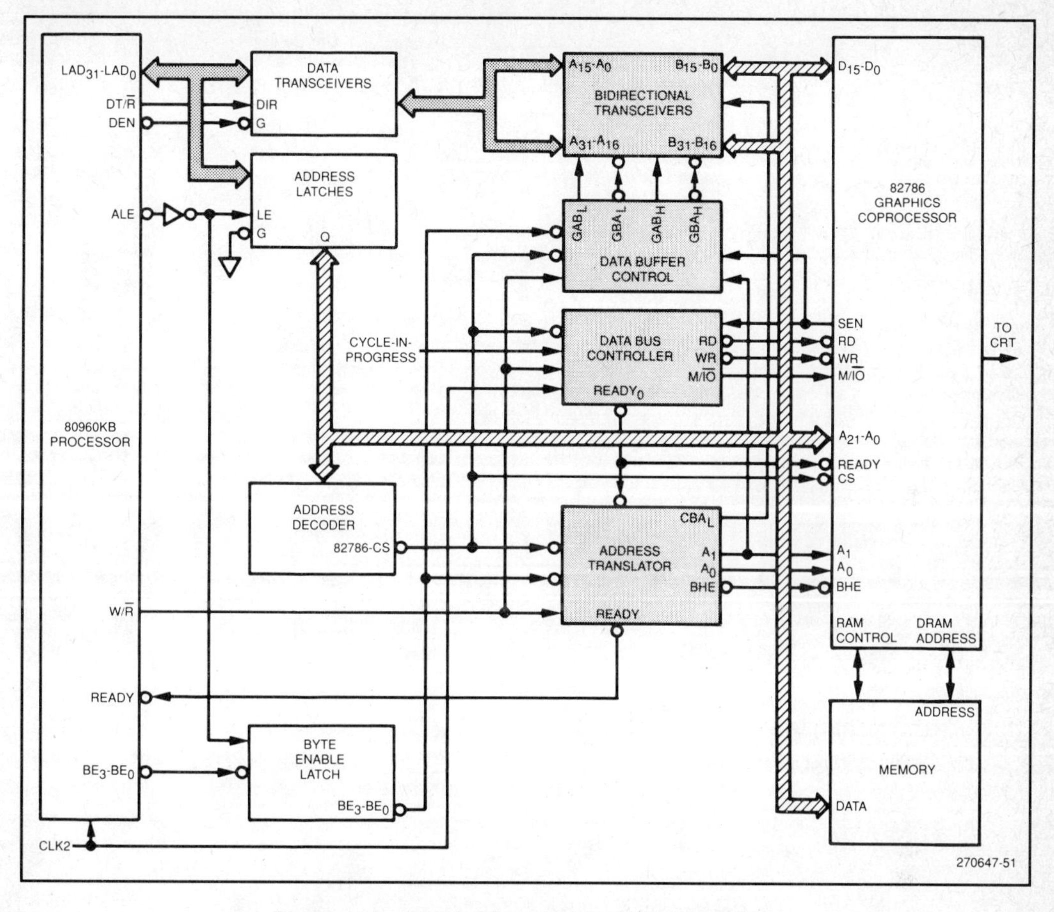

Figure 5-6: Block Diagram for 82786 Interface

The address translator performs four functions:

1. Converts four byte enable signals to A_0, A_1, and $\overline{BHE}$.
2. Increments A_1 after receiving $\overline{READY}$ for the first 16-bit transfer.
3. Generates the clock signal ($\overline{CBA_L}$) that latches the first 16-bit data word in the bidirectional transceivers when the 80960KB processor performs a read operation.
4. Generates the $\overline{READY}$ signal for the CPU.

Not shown is the cycle detector circuit that generates the CYCLE-IN-PROGRESS signal. This signal can be generated by using the circuit similar to the one shown in Figure 5-2. Logic gates the $\overline{ADS}$ and $\overline{DEN}$ signals to start the cycle. The same logic asserts the $\overline{READY}$ signal at the end of the cycle.

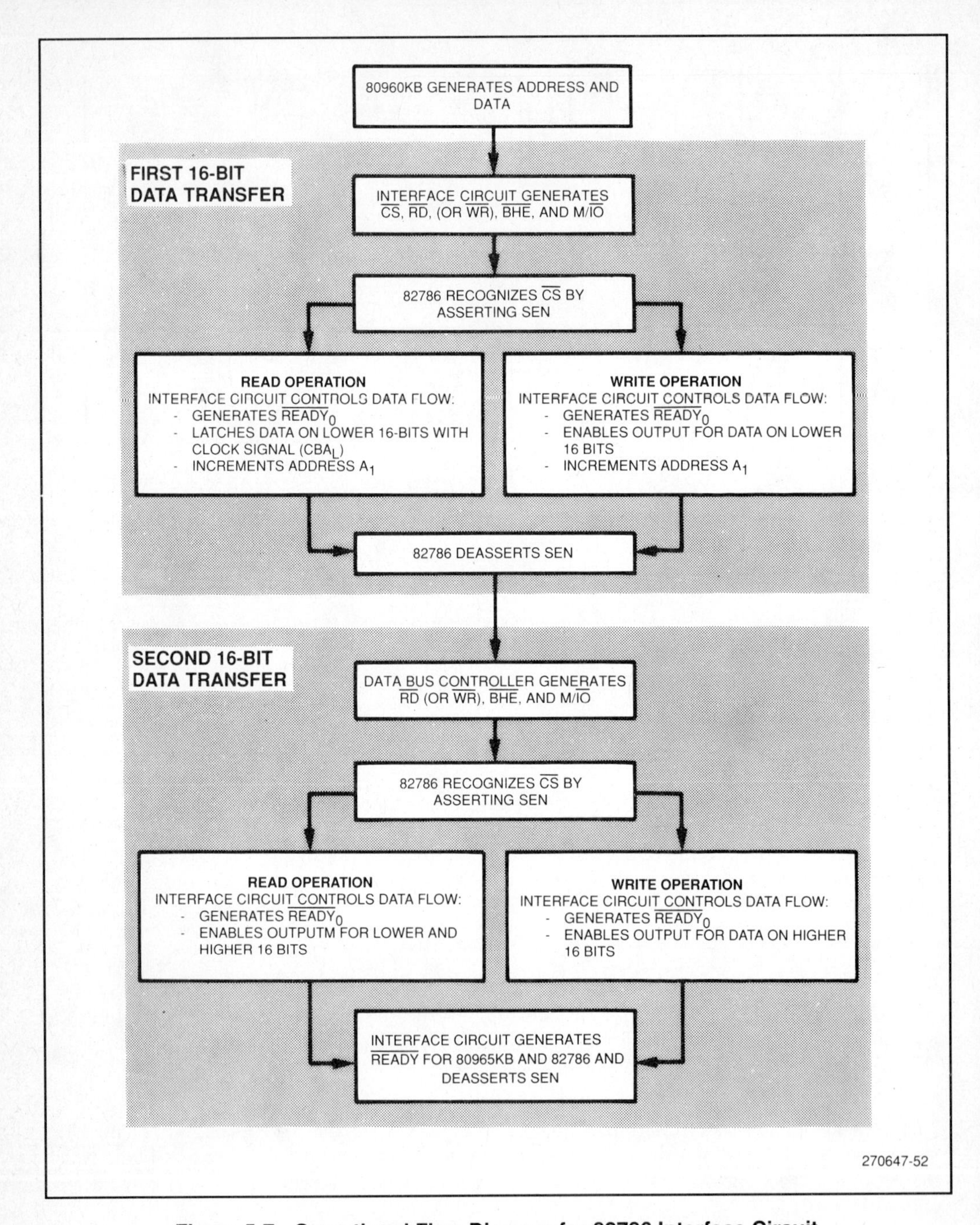

Figure 5-7: Operational Flow Diagram for 82786 Interface Circuit

5.3.10 Operation

Figure 5-7 illustrates the interaction between the 82786 and the 80960KB processor. The operation is divided into two 16-bit data movements for both a read and write operation.

The 80960KB processor generates a memory-mapped address and data for the desired graphics memory location to access the 82786. The processor triggers the interface circuit to generate the chip select signal and the following operational signals: the read ($\overline{RD}$) or write ($\overline{WR}$) command, $\overline{BHE}$, and the memory or I/O (M/$\overline{IO}$) signal. The 82786 begins the memory operation after it completes the current graphics processing activity. The 82786 asserts SEN to acknowledge that it is performing a memory operation.

After the 82786 asserts SEN, it begins a 16-bit memory read or write operation. The 82786 translates the address inputs (A_{21} through A) to a multiplexed DRAM address, and generates the DRAM control signals. Note that signals A_1 and A derive from the byte enable signals.

For a read operation, the data bus controller uses SEN to generate the $\overline{READY}$ signal. The assertion of $\overline{READY}$ causes the address translator to increment A_1 and to generate $\overline{CBA_L}$, which latches the lower 16 data bits on the B inputs of the bidirectional transceivers to the A side.

Similarly, for a write operation, the data bus controller uses SEN to generate the $\overline{READY}$ signal. The assertion of $\overline{READY}$ causes the address translator to increment A_1. The data buffer control uses SEN and the byte enable signals to produce $\overline{GAB_L}$, which enables the outputs for the lower 16 data bits of the bidirectional transceivers.

The 82786 then deasserts SEN to complete the transfer of the first 16 data bits. To transfer the second 16 data bits, the interface circuit generates $\overline{RD}$ (or $\overline{WR}$), $\overline{BHE}$, and M/$\overline{IO}$ ($\overline{CS}$ is already asserted) to request another memory operation. After it completes the current graphics processing activity, the 82786 begins the memory operation and asserts SEN.

For a read operation, the data bus controller uses SEN to generate the $\overline{READY}$ signal. The data buffer control uses SEN to assert $\overline{GBA_H}$ and $\overline{GBA_L}$, which enables the outputs for the higher and lower 16 data bits.

For a write operation, the data bus controller uses SEN to generate the $\overline{READY}$ signal. The data buffer control uses SEN and the byte enable signals to produce $\overline{GAB_H}$, which enables the outputs for the higher 16 data bits of the bidirectional transceivers.

The address translator generates $\overline{READY}$ for the 80960KB processor from the second $\overline{READY}$ to terminate the transfer of data to the graphics memory.

5.4 SUMMARY

The 80960KB processor supports 8-bit, 16-bit, and 32-bit I/O interfaces. A general system interface circuit can be designed to connect to many slave-type peripherals. You can later expand this interface to accommodate a bus master peripheral or a 32-bit to 16-bit data bus translator.

INDEX

82530/80960KB Interface 5-7, 5-8
82586/80960KB Interface 5-9
8259A/80960KB Interface 5-5
82786/80960KB Interface 5-12

A

Address Decoder
- I/O interface 5-1
- memory interface 4-1

Address Latch/Demultiplexer
- I/O interface 5-1
- memory interface 4-1

ADS (Address/Data Status) Signal
- definition 3-4
- timing diagram 3-9
- used by the 82786 interface 5-15
- used by the burst logic 4-3
- used by the timing control logic 5-4

ALE (Address Latch Enable) Signal
- definition 3-4
- timing diagram 3-8
- used by an address latch/demultiplexer 4-2, 5-3
- used by the byte enable latch 4-10
- used by the SRAM interface logic 4-14
- used in the SRAM interface logic 4-15

Arbitration
- L-bus example 3-23
- protocol for the L-bus 3-17
- timing on the L-bus 3-19

B

BADAC (Bad Access) Signal 3-37

BE_3-BE_0 (Byte Enable) Signals
- definition 3-4
- timing 3-5
- timing diagram 3-9
- used by the byte enable latch 4-10
- used by the DRAM controller 4-20

Burst Logic
- memory interface 4-6
- signal flow 4-7

Burst Transaction 3-11

C

CACHE Signal 3-6

CLK2 (Processor Clock) or CLK (Bus Clock)
- CLK2 requirements 3-14
- generation 3-15
- relationship of CLK2 and CLK 3-8

C (con't)

CYCLE-IN-PROCESS Signal
- definition 4-6
- used by the burst logic 4-6
- used by the DRAM arbiter 4-17
- used by the DRAM timing and control 4-18, 4-20

D

Data Transceivers
- I/O interface 5-3
- memory interface 4-1

DEN (Data Enable) Signal
- definition 3-4
- timing diagram 3-10
- used by a data transceiver 4-1, 5-3
- used by the burst logic 4-6

DRAM Address Multiplexer 4-16
DRAM Arbiter 4-17
DRAM Controller 4-15
DRAM Interleaving 4-19
DRAM Refresh Interval Timer 4-17
DRAM Timing and Control 4-17
DRAM Timing Considerations 4-20

DT/R (data Transmit/Receive) Signal
- definition 3-4
- timing diagram 3-9
- used by a data transceiver 4-1, 5-3
- used by the 82586 interface 5-10, 5-11

F

FAILURE Signal 3-44

H

HLDA (Hold Acknowledge) Signal 3-18
HLDAR (Hold Acknowledge Request) Signal 3-21
HOLD Signal 3-18
HOLDR (Hold Request) Signal 3-21

I

I/O Address Range 5-3
I/O Interface to 8-bit and 16 bit Peripherals 5-1
I/O Interface to the 80960KB 5-1
Initialization for 80960KB 3-41

I (con't)
INT_0/IAC (Interrupt$_0$ or Inter-Agent Communication)
  Signal 3-29
INT_1 (Interrupt$_1$) Signal 3-29
INT_2/INTR (Interrupt$_2$ or Interrupt Request) Signal 3-29
INT_3/INTA (Interrupt$_3$ or Interrupt Acknowledge)
  Signal 3-29
Interrupts
  definition 3-29
  direct interrupt pins 3-31
  Interrupt Control register 3-31
  pins that interface to an interrupt controller 3-31
  signals 3-29
  synchronization 3-33
  timing diagram 3-32

L
L-Bus States
  address (T_a) 3-21, 3-1
  data (T_d) 3-21, 3-1
  hold (T_h) 3-19
  hold request (T_{hr}) 3-21
  idle (T_i) 3-21, 3-1
  recovery (T_r) 3-21, 3-1
  wait (T_w) 3-21, 3-1
LAD (Local Address/Data) lines 3-4, 3-3
LAD_1-LAD_0
  See SIZE Signals
LOCK Signal
  definition 3-6
  used during arbitration 3-21

M
Memory Address Range 4-5
Memory Interface to the 80960KB 4-1

P
PBM (Primary Bus Master) 3-20

R
Read Operation, timing diagram for the L-bus 3-8
READY Signal
  definition 3-6
  timing diagram 3-9
  used by the 82530 interface 5-9
  used by the 82586 interface 5-11
  used by the 8259A interface 5-7
  used by the 82786 interface 5-15
  used by the byte enable latch 4-10
  used by the SRAM interface 4-13, 4-14, 4-15
  used by the timing control logic 4-5, 5-4

R (con't)
RESET
  timing generation for 80960KB 3-40
  timing requirements for 80960KB 3-40

S
SBM (Secondary Bus Master) 3-21
SIZE Signals
  definition 3-3
  used by the 82586 interface 5-11
  used by the burst logic 4-6
SRAM Interface
  interface logic 4-9
  timing considerations 4-11

T
Timing
  arbitration on the L-bus 3-20
  interrupts 3-31
  read operation on the L-bus 3-8
  write operation on the L-bus 3-9
Timing Logic
  I/O interface 5-3
  signal flow 4-5

W
W/R (Write/Read) Signal
  definition 3-4
  timing diagram 3-8
  used by the 82530 interface 5-9
  used by the 82786 interface 5-12
  used by the DRAM timing control logic 4-17
  used by the timing control logic 5-4, 4-5
Write Operation, timing diagram on the L-bus 3-10

DOMESTIC SALES OFFICES

ALABAMA

†Intel Corp.
5015 Bradford Dr., #2
Huntsville 35805
Tel: (205) 830-4010

ARIZONA

†Intel Corp.
11225 N. 28th Dr.
Suite D-214
Phoenix 85029
Tel: (602) 869-4980

Intel Corp.
1161 N. El Dorado Place
Suite 301
Tucson 85715
Tel: (602) 299-6815

CALIFORNIA

†Intel Corp.
21515 Vanowen Street
Suite 116
Canoga Park 91303
Tel: (818) 704-8500

†Intel Corp.
2250 E. Imperial Highway
Suite 218
El Segundo 90245
Tel: (213) 640-6040

Intel Corp.
1510 Arden Way, Suite 101
Sacramento 95815
Tel: (916) 920-8096

Intel Corp.
9665 Chesapeake Dr.
Suite 325
San Diego 95123
Tel: (619) 292-8086

†Intel Corp.*
400 N. Tustin Avenue
Suite 450
Santa Ana 92705
Tel: (714) 835-9642
TWX: 910-595-1114

†Intel Corp.*
San Tomas 4
2700 San Tomas Expressway
2nd Floor
Santa Clara 95051
Tel: (408) 986-8086
TWX: 910-338-0255
FAX: 408-727-2620

COLORADO

Intel Corp.
4445 Northpark Drive
Suite 100
Colorado Springs 80907
Tel: (719) 594-6622

†Intel Corp.*
650 S. Cherry St., Suite 915
Denver 80222
Tel: (303) 321-8086
TWX: 910-931-2289

CONNECTICUT

†Intel Corp.
26 Mill Plain Road
2nd Floor
Danbury 06811
Tel: (203) 748-3130
TWX: 710-456-1199

FLORIDA

†Intel Corp.
6363 N.W. 6th Way, Suite 100
Ft. Lauderdale 33309
Tel: (305) 771-0600
TWX: 510-956-9407
FAX: 305-772-8193

†Intel Corp.
5850 T.G. Lee Blvd.
Suite 340
Orlando 32822
Tel: (407) 240-8000
FAX: 407-240-8097

Intel Corp.
11300 4th Street North
Suite 170
St. Petersburg 33716
Tel: (813) 577-2413
FAX: 813-578-1607

GEORGIA

Intel Corp.
20 Technology Parkway, N.W.
Suite 150
Norcross 30092
Tel: (404) 449-0541

ILLINOIS

†Intel Corp.*
300 N. Martingale Road, Suite 400
Schaumburg 60173
Tel: (312) 605-8031
FAX: 312-605-9762

INDIANA

†Intel Corp.
8777 Purdue Road
Suite 125
Indianapolis 46268
Tel: (317) 875-0623

IOWA

Intel Corp.
1930 St. Andrews Drive N.E.
2nd Floor
Cedar Rapids 52402
Tel: (319) 393-5510

KANSAS

†Intel Corp.
10985 Cody St.
Suite 140, Bldg. D
Overland Park 66210
Tel: (913) 345-2727

MARYLAND

Intel Corp.*
7321 Parkway Drive South
Suite C
Hanover 21076
Tel: (301) 796-7500
TWX: 710-862-1944

†Intel Corp.
7833 Walker Drive
Suite 550
Greenbelt 20770
Tel: (301) 441-1020

MASSACHUSETTS

†Intel Corp.*
Westford Corp. Center
3 Carlisle Road
2nd Floor
Westford 01886
Tel: (508) 692-3222
TWX: 710-343-6333

MICHIGAN

†Intel Corp.
7071 Orchard Lake Road
Suite 100
West Bloomfield 48322
Tel: (313) 851-8096

MINNESOTA

†Intel Corp.
3500 W. 80th St., Suite 360
Bloomington 55431
Tel: (612) 835-6722
TWX: 910-576-2867

MISSOURI

†Intel Corp.
4203 Earth City Expressway
Suite 131
Earth City 63045
Tel: (314) 291-1990

NEW JERSEY

†Intel Corp.*
Parkway 109 Office Center
328 Newman Springs Road
Red Bank 07701
Tel: (201) 747-2233

†Intel Corp.
280 Corporate Center
75 Livingston Avenue
First Floor
Roseland 07068
Tel: (201) 740-0111
FAX: 201-740-0626

NEW YORK

Intel Corp.*
850 Cross Keys Office Park
Fairport 14450
Tel: (716) 425-2750
TWX: 510-253-7391

†Intel Corp.*
2950 Expressway Dr., South
Suite 130
Islandia 11722
Tel: (516) 231-3300
TWX: 510-227-6236

†Intel Corp.
Westage Business Center
Bldg. 300, Route 9
Fishkill 12524
Tel: (914) 897-3860
FAX: 914-897-3125

NORTH CAROLINA

†Intel Corp.
5800 Executive Center Dr.
Suite 105
Charlotte 28212
Tel: (704) 568-8966
FAX: 704-535-2236

†Intel Corp.
2700 Wycliff Road
Suite 102
Raleigh 27607
Tel: (919) 851-9537

OHIO

†Intel Corp.*
3401 Park Center Drive
Suite 220
Dayton 45414
Tel: (513) 890-5350
TWX: 810-450-2528

†Intel Corp.*
25700 Science Park Dr., Suite 100
Beachwood 44122
Tel: (216) 464-2736
TWX: 810-427-9298

OKLAHOMA

Intel Corp.
6801 N. Broadway
Suite 115
Oklahoma City 73162
Tel: (405) 848-8086

OREGON

†Intel Corp.
15254 N.W. Greenbrier Parkway
Building B
Beaverton 97005
Tel: (503) 645-8051
TWX: 910-467-8741

PENNSYLVANIA

†Intel Corp.*
455 Pennsylvania Avenue
Suite 230
Fort Washington 19034
Tel: (215) 641-1000
TWX: 510-661-2077

†Intel Corp.*
400 Penn Center Blvd., Suite 610
Pittsburgh 15235
Tel: (412) 823-4970

PUERTO RICO

†Intel Microprocessor Corp.
South Industrial Park
P.O. Box 910
Las Piedras 00671
Tel: (809) 733-8616

TEXAS

†Intel Corp.
313 E. Anderson Lane
Suite 314
Austin 78752
Tel: (512) 343-2435

†Intel Corp.*
12000 Ford Road
Suite 400
Dallas 75234
Tel: (214) 241-8087
FAX: 214-484-1180

†Intel Corp.*
7322 S.W. Freeway
Suite 1490
Houston 77074
Tel: (713) 988-8086
TWX: 910-881-2490

UTAH

†Intel Corp.
428 East 6400 South
Suite 104
Murray 84107
Tel: (801) 263-8051

VIRGINIA

†Intel Corp.
1504 Santa Rosa Road
Suite 108
Richmond 23288
Tel: (804) 282-5668

WASHINGTON

†Intel Corp.
155 108th Avenue N.E.
Suite 386
Bellevue 98004
Tel: (206) 453-8086
TWX: 910-443-3002

Intel Corp.
408 N. Mullan Road
Suite 102
Spokane 99206
Tel: (509) 928-8086

WISCONSIN

Intel Corp.
330 S. Executive Dr.
Suite 102
Brookfield 53005
Tel: (414) 784-8087
FAX: (414) 796-2115

CANADA

BRITISH COLUMBIA

†Intel Semiconductor of Canada, Ltd.
4585 Canada Way, Suite 202
Burnaby V5G 4L6
Tel: (604) 298-0387
FAX: (604) 298-8234

ONTARIO

†Intel Semiconductor of Canada, Ltd.
2650 Queensview Drive
Suite 250
Ottawa K2B 8H6
Tel: (613) 829-9714
FAX: 613-820-5936

†Intel Semiconductor of Canada, Ltd.
190 Attwell Drive
Suite 500
Rexdale M9W 6H8
Tel: (416) 675-2105
TLX: 06983574
FAX: (416) 675-2438

QUEBEC

†Intel Semiconductor of Canada, Ltd.
620 St. John Boulevard
Pointe Claire H9R 3K2
Tel: (514) 694-9130
FAX: 514-694-0064

†Sales and Service Office
*Field Application Location

CG/SALE/052289

DOMESTIC DISTRIBUTORS

ALABAMA

Arrow Electronics, Inc.
1015 Henderson Road
Huntsville 35805
Tel: (205) 837-6955

†Hamilton/Avnet Electronics
4940 Research Drive
Huntsville 35805
Tel: (205) 837-7210
TWX: 810-726-2162

Pioneer/Technologies Group, Inc.
4825 University Square
Huntsville 35805
Tel: (205) 837-9300
TWX: 810-726-2197

ARIZONA

†Hamilton/Avnet Electronics
505 S. Madison Drive
Tempe 85281
Tel: (602) 231-5140
TWX: 910-950-0077

Hamilton/Avnet Electronics
30 South McKiemy
Chandler 85226
Tel: (602) 961-6669
TWX: 910-950-0077

Arrow Electronics, Inc.
4134 E. Wood Street
Phoenix 85040
Tel: (602) 437-0750
TWX: 910-951-1550

Wyle Distribution Group
17855 N. Black Canyon Hwy.
Phoenix 85023
Tel: (602) 249-2232
TWX: 910-951-4282

CALIFORNIA

Arrow Electronics, Inc.
10824 Hope Street
Cypress 90630
Tel: (714) 220-6300

Arrow Electronics, Inc.
19748 Dearborn Street
Chatsworth 91311
Tel: (213) 701-7500
TWX: 910-493-2086

†Arow Electronics, Inc.
521 Weddell Drive
Sunnyvale 94086
Tel: (408) 745-6600
TWX: 910-339-9371

Arrow Electronics, Inc.
9511 Ridgehaven Court
San Diego 92123
Tel: (619) 565-4800
TWX: 888-064

†Arrow Electronics, Inc.
2961 Dow Avenue
Tustin 92680
Tel: (714) 838-5422
TWX: 910-595-2860

†Avnet Electronics
350 McCormick Avenue
Costa Mesa 92626
Tel: (714) 754-6071
TWX: 910-595-1928

†Hamilton/Avnet Electronics
1175 Bordeaux Drive
Sunnyvale 94086
Tel: (408) 743-3300
TWX: 910-339-9332

†Hamilton/Avnet Electronics
4545 Ridgeview Avenue
San Diego 92123
Tel: (619) 571-7500
TWX: 910-595-2638

†Hamilton/Avnet Electronics
9650 Desoto Avenue
Chatsworth 91311
Tel: (818) 700-1161

†Hamilton Electro Sales
10950 W. Washington Blvd.
Culver City 20230
Tel: (213) 558-2458
TWX: 910-340-6364

Hamilton Electro Sales
1361B West 190th Street
Gardena 90248
Tel: (213) 217-6700

†Hamilton/Avnet Electronics
3002 'G' Street
Ontario 91761
Tel: (714) 989-9411

†Avnet Electronics
20501 Plummer
Chatsworth 91351
Tel: (213) 700-6271
TWX: 910-494-2207

†Hamilton Electro Sales
3170 Pullman Street
Costa Mesa 92626
Tel: (714) 641-4150
TWX: 910-595-2638

†Hamilton/Avnet Electronics
4103 Northgate Blvd.
Sacramento 95834
Tel: (916) 920-3150

Wyle Distribution Group
124 Maryland Street
El Segundo 90254
Tel: (213) 322-8100

Wyle Distribution Group
7382 Lampson Ave.
Garden Grove 92641
Tel: (714) 891-1717
TWX: 910-348-7140 or 7111

Wyle Distribution Group
11151 Sun Center Drive
Rancho Cordova 95670
Tel: (916) 638-5282

†Wyle Distribution Group
9525 Chesapeake Drive
San Diego 92123
Tel: (619) 565-9171
TWX: 910-335-1590

†Wyle Distribution Group
3000 Bowers Avenue
Santa Clara 95051
Tel: (408) 727-2500
TWX: 910-338-0296

†Wyle Distribution Group
17872 Cowan Avenue
Irvine 92714
Tel: (714) 863-9953
TWX: 910-595-1572

Wyle Distribution Group
26677 W. Agoura Rd.
Calabasas 91302
Tel: (818) 880-9000
TWX: 372-0232

COLORADO

Arrow Electronics, Inc.
7060 South Tucson Way
Englewood 80112
Tel: (303) 790-4444

†Hamilton/Avnet Electronics
8765 E. Orchard Road
Suite 708
Englewood 80111
Tel: (303) 740-1017
TWX: 910-935-0787

†Wyle Distribution Group
451 E. 124th Avenue
Thornton 80241
Tel: (303) 457-9953
TWX: 910-936-0770

CONNECTICUT

†Arrow Electronics, Inc.
12 Beaumont Road
Wallingford 06492
Tel: (203) 265-7741
TWX: 710-476-0162

Hamilton/Avnet Electronics
Commerce Industrial Park
Commerce Drive
Danbury 06810
Tel: (203) 797-2800
TWX: 710-456-9974

†Pioneer Electronics
112 Main Street
Norwalk 06851
Tel: (203) 853-1515
TWX: 710-468-3373

FLORIDA

†Arrow Electronics, Inc.
400 Fairway Drive
Suite 102
Deerfield Beach 33441
Tel: (305) 429-8200
TWX: 510-955-9456

Arrow Electronics, Inc.
37 Skyline Drive
Suite 3101
Lake Marv 32746
Tel: (407) 323-0252
TWX: 510-959-6337

†Hamilton/Avnet Electronics
6801 N.W. 15th Way
Ft. Lauderdale 33309
Tel: (305) 971-2900
TWX: 510-956-3097

†Hamilton/Avnet Electronics
3197 Tech Drive North
St. Petersburg 33702
Tel: (813) 576-3930
TWX: 810-863-0374

†Hamilton/Avnet Electronics
6947 University Boulevard
Winter Park 32792
Tel: (305) 628-3888
TWX: 810-853-0322

†Pioneer/Technologies Group, Inc.
337 S. Lake Blvd.
Alta Monte Springs 32701
Tel: (407) 834-9090
TWX: 810-853-0284

Pioneer/Technologies Group, Inc.
674 S. Military Trail
Deerfield Beach 33442
Tel: (305) 428-8877
TWX: 510-955-9653

GEORGIA

†Arrow Electronics, Inc.
3155 Northwoods Parkway
Suite A
Norcross 30071
Tel: (404) 449-8252
TWX: 810-766-0439

†Hamilton/Avnet Electronics
5825 D Peachtree Corners
Norcross 30092
Tel: (404) 447-7500
TWX: 810-766-0432

Pioneer/Technologies Group, Inc.
3100 F Northwoods Place
Norcross 30071
Tel: (404) 448-1711
TWX: 810-766-4515

ILLINOIS

Arrow Electronics, Inc.
1140 W. Thorndale
Itasca 60143
Tel: (312) 250-0500
TWX: 312-250-0916

†Hamilton/Avnet Electronics
1130 Thorndale Avenue
Bensenville 60106
Tel: (312) 860-7780
TWX: 910-227-0060

MTI Systems Sales
1100 W. Thorndale
Itasca 60143
Tel: (312) 773-2300

†Pioneer Electronics
1551 Carmen Drive
Elk Grove Village 60007
Tel: (312) 437-9680
TWX: 910-222-1834

INDIANA

†Arrow Electronics, Inc.
2495 Directors Row, Suite H
Indianapolis 46241
Tel: (317) 243-9353
TWX: 810-341-3119

Hamilton/Avnet Electronics
485 Gradle Drive
Carmel 46032
Tel: (317) 844-9333
TWX: 810-260-3966

†Pioneer Electronics
6408 Castleplace Drive
Indianapolis 46250
Tel: (317) 849-7300
TWX: 810-260-1794

IOWA

Hamilton/Avnet Electronics
915 33rd Avenue, S.W.
Cedar Rapids 52404
Tel: (319) 362-4757

KANSAS

Arrow Electronics
8208 Melrose Dr., Suite 210
Lenexa 66214
Tel: (913) 541-9542

†Hamilton/Avnet Electronics
9219 Quivera Road
Overland Park 66215
Tel: (913) 888-8900
TWX: 910-743-0005

Pioneer/Tec Gr.
10551 Lockman Rd.
Lenexa 66215
Tel: (913) 492-0500

KENTUCKY

Hamilton/Avnet Electronics
1051 D. Newton Park
Lexington 40511
Tel: (606) 259-1475

MARYLAND

Arrow Electronics, Inc.
8300 Guilford Drive
Suite H, River Center
Columbia 21046
Tel: (301) 995-0003
TWX: 710-236-9005

Hamilton/Avnet Electronics
6822 Oak Hall Lane
Columbia 21045
Tel: (301) 995-3500
TWX: 710-862-1861

†Mesa Technology Corp.
9720 Patuxent Woods Dr.
Columbia 21046
Tel: (301) 290-8150
TWX: 710-828-9702

†Pioneer/Technologies Group, Inc.
9100 Gaither Road
Gaithersburg 20877
Tel: (301) 921-0660
TWX: 710-828-0545

MASSACHUSETTS

Arrow Electronics, Inc.
25 Upton Dr.
Wilmington 01887
Tel: (617) 935-5134

†Hamilton/Avnet Electronics
10D Centennial Drive
Peabody 01960
Tel: (617) 531-7430
TWX: 710-393-0382

MTI Systems Sales
83 Cambridge St.
Burlington 01813

Pioneer Electronics
44 Hartwell Avenue
Lexington 02173
Tel: (617) 861-9200
TWX: 710-326-6617

MICHIGAN

Arrow Electronics, Inc.
755 Phoenix Drive
Ann Arbor 48104
Tel: (313) 971-8220
TWX: 810-223-6020

Hamilton/Avnet Electronics
2215 29th Street S.E.
Space A5
Grand Rapids 49508
Tel: (616) 243-8805
TWX: 810-274-6921

Pioneer Electronics
4504 Broadmoor S.E.
Grand Rapids 49508
FAX: 616-698-1831

†Hamilton/Avnet Electronics
32487 Schoolcraft Road
Livonia 48150
Tel: (313) 522-4700
TWX: 810-282-8775

†Pioneer/Michigan
13485 Stamford
Livonia 48150
Tel: (313) 525-1800
TWX: 810-242-3271

MINNESOTA

†Arrow Electronics, Inc.
5230 W. 73rd Street
Edina 55435
Tel: (612) 830-1800
TWX: 910-576-3125

†Hamilton/Avnet Electronics
12400 Whitewater Drive
Minnetonka 55434
Tel: (612) 932-0600

†Pioneer Electronics
7625 Golden Triange Dr.
Suite G
Eden Prairi 55343
Tel: (612) 944-3355

MISSOURI

†Arrow Electronics, Inc.
2380 Schuetz
St. Louis 63141
Tel: (314) 567-6888
TWX: 910-764-0882

†Hamilton/Avnet Electronics
13743 Shoreline Court
Earth City 63045
Tel: (314) 344-1200
TWX: 910-762-0684

NEW HAMPSHIRE

†Arrow Electronics, Inc.
3 Perimeter Road
Manchester 03103
Tel: (603) 668-6968
TWX: 710-220-1684

†Hamilton/Avnet Electronics
444 E. Industrial Drive
Manchester 03103
Tel: (603) 624-9400

†Microcomputer System Technical Distributor Center

DOMESTIC DISTRIBUTORS (Cont'd.)

NEW JERSEY

†Arrow Electronics, Inc.
Four East Stow Road
Unit 11
Marlton 08053
Tel: (609) 596-8000
TWX: 710-897-0829

†Arrow Electronics
6 Century Drive
Parsipanny 07054
Tel: (201) 538-0900

†Hamilton/Avnet Electronics
1 Keystone Ave., Bldg. 36
Cherry Hill 08003
Tel: (609) 424-0110
TWX: 710-940-0262

†Hamilton/Avnet Electronics
10 Industrial
Fairfield 07006
Tel: (201) 575-5300
TWX: 710-734-4388

†MTI Systems Sales
37 Kulick Rd.
Fairfield 07006
Tel: (201) 227-5552

†Pioneer Electronics
45 Route 46
Pinebrook 07058
Tel: (201) 575-3510
TWX: 710-734-4382

NEW MEXICO

Alliance Electronics Inc.
11030 Cochiti S.E.
Albuquerque 87123
Tel: (505) 292-3360
TWX: 910-989-1151

Hamilton/Avnet Electronics
2524 Baylor Drive S.E.
Albuquerque 87106
Tel: (505) 765-1500
TWX: 910-989-0614

NEW YORK

†Arrow Electronics, Inc.
3375 Brighton Henrietta
Townline Rd.
Rochester 14623
Tel: (716) 275-0300
TWX: 510-253-4766

Arrow Electronics, Inc.
20 Oser Avenue
Hauppauge 11788
Tel: (516) 231-1000
TWX: 510-227-6623

Hamilton/Avnet
933 Motor Parkway
Hauppauge 11788
Tel: (516) 231-9800
TWX: 510-224-6166

†Hamilton/Avnet Electronics
333 Metro Park
Rochester 14623
Tel: (716) 475-9130
TWX: 510-253-5470

†Hamilton/Avnet Electronics
103 Twin Oaks Drive
Syracuse 13206
Tel: (315) 437-0288
TWX: 710-541-1560

†MTI Systems Sales
38 Harbor Park Drive
Port Washington 11050
Tel: (516) 621-6200

†Pioneer Electronics
68 Corporate Drive
Binghamton 13904
Tel: (607) 722-9300
TWX: 510-252-0893

Pioneer Electronics
40 Oser Avenue
Hauppauge 11787
Tel: (516) 231-9200

†Pioneer Electronics
60 Crossway Park West
Woodbury, Long Island 11797
Tel: (516) 921-8700
TWX: 510-221-2184

†Pioneer Electronics
840 Fairport Park
Fairport 14450
Tel: (716) 381-7070
TWX: 510-253-7001

NORTH CAROLINA

†Arrow Electronics, Inc.
5240 Greensdairy Road
Raleigh 27604
Tel: (919) 876-3132
TWX: 510-928-1856

†Hamilton/Avnet Electronics
3510 Spring Forest Drive
Raleigh 27604
Tel: (919) 878-0819
TWX: 510-928-1836

Pioneer/Technologies Group, Inc.
9801 A-Southern Pine Blvd.
Charlotte 28210
Tel: (919) 527-8188
TWX: 810-621-0366

OHIO

Arrow Electronics, Inc.
7620 McEwen Road
Centerville 45459
Tel: (513) 435-5563
TWX: 810-459-1611

†Arrow Electronics, Inc.
6236 Cochran Road
Solon 44139
Tel: (216) 248-3990
TWX: 810-427-9409

†Hamilton/Avnet Electronics
954 Senate Drive
Dayton 45459
Tel: (513) 439-6733
TWX: 810-450-2531

Hamilton/Avnet Electronics
4588 Emery Industrial Pkwy.
Warrensville Heights 44128
Tel: (216) 349-5100
TWX: 810-427-9452

†Hamilton/Avnet Electronics
777 Brooksedge Blvd.
Westerville 43081
Tel: (614) 882-7004

†Pioneer Electronics
4433 Interpoint Boulevard
Dayton 45424
Tel: (513) 236-9900
TWX: 810-459-1622

†Pioneer Electronics
4800 E. 131st Street
Cleveland 44105
Tel: (216) 587-3600
TWX: 810-422-2211

OKLAHOMA

Arrow Electronics, Inc.
1211 E. 51st St., Suite 101
Tulsa 74146
Tel: (918) 252-7537

†Hamilton/Avnet Electronics
12121 E. 51st St., Suite 102A
Tulsa 74146
Tel: (918) 252-7297

OREGON

†Almac Electronics Corp.
1885 N.W. 169th Place
Beaverton 97005
Tel: (503) 629-8090
TWX: 910-467-8746

†Hamilton/Avnet Electronics
6024 S.W. Jean Road
Bldg. C, Suite 10
Lake Oswego 97034
Tel: (503) 635-7848
TWX: 910-455-8179

Wyle Distribution Group
5250 N.E. Elam Young Parkway
Suite 600
Hillsboro 97124
Tel: (503) 640-6000
TWX: 910-460-2203

PENNSYLVANIA

Arrow Electronics, Inc.
650 Seco Road
Monroeville 15146
Tel: (412) 856-7000

Hamilton/Avnet Electronics
2800 Liberty Ave.
Pittsburgh 15238
Tel: (412) 281-4150

Pioneer Electronics
259 Kappa Drive
Pittsburgh 15238
Tel: (412) 782-2300
TWX: 710-795-3122

†Pioneer/Technologies Group, Inc.
Delaware Valley
261 Gibralter Road
Horsham 19044
Tel: (215) 674-4000
TWX: 510-665-6778

TEXAS

†Arrow Electronics, Inc.
3220 Commander Drive
Carrollton 75006
Tel: (214) 380-6464
TWX: 910-860-5377

†Arrow Electronics, Inc.
10899 Kinghurst
Suite 100
Houston 77099
Tel: (713) 530-4700
TWX: 910-880-4439

†Arrow Electronics, Inc.
2227 W. Braker Lane
Austin 78758
Tel: (512) 835-4180
TWX: 910-874-1348

†Hamilton/Avnet Electronics
1807 W. Braker Lane
Austin 78758
Tel: (512) 837-8911
TWX: 910-874-1319

†Hamilton/Avnet Electronics
2111 W. Walnut Hill Lane
Irving 75038
Tel: (214) 550-6111
TWX: 910-860-5929

†Hamilton/Avnet Electronics
4850 Wright Rd., Suite 190
Stafford 77477
Tel: (713) 240-7733
TWX: 910-881-5523

†Pioneer Electronics
18260 Kramer
Austin 78758
Tel: (512) 835-4000
TWX: 910-874-1323

†Pioneer Electronics
13710 Omega Road
Dallas 75234
Tel: (214) 386-7300
TWX: 910-850-5563

†Pioneer Electronics
5853 Point West Drive
Houston 77036
Tel: (713) 988-5555
TWX: 910-881-1606

Wyle Distribution Group
1810 Greenville Avenue
Richardson 75081
Tel: (214) 235-9953

UTAH

Arrow Electronics
1946 Parkway Blvd.
Salt Lake City 84119
Tel: (801) 973-6913

†Hamilton/Avnet Electronics
1585 West 2100 South
Salt Lake City 84119
Tel: (801) 972-2800
TWX: 910-925-4018

Wyle Distribution Group
1325 West 2200 South
Suite E
West Valley 84119
Tel: (801) 974-9953

WASHINGTON

†Almac Electronics Corp.
14360 S.E. Eastgate Way
Bellevue 98007
Tel: (206) 643-9992
TWX: 910-444-2067

Arrow Electronics, Inc.
19540 68th Ave. South
Kent 98032
Tel: (206) 575-4420

†Hamilton/Avnet Electronics
14212 N.E. 21st Street
Bellevue 98005
Tel: (206) 643-3950
TWX: 910-443-2469

Wyle Distribution Group
15385 N.E. 90th Street
Redmond 98052
Tel: (206) 881-1150

WISCONSIN

Arrow Electronics, Inc.
200 N. Patrick Blvd., Ste. 100
Brookfield 53005
Tel: (414) 767-6600
TWX: 910-262-1193

Hamilton/Avnet Electronics
2975 Moorland Road
New Berlin 53151
Tel: (414) 784-4510
TWX: 910-262-1182

CANADA

ALBERTA

Hamilton/Avnet Electronics
2816 21st Street N.E.
Calgary T2E 6Z3
Tel: (403) 230-3586
TWX: 03-827-642

Zentronics
Bay No. 1
3300 14th Avenue N.E.
Calgary T2A 6J4
Tel: (403) 272-1021

BRITISH COLUMBIA

†Hamilton/Avnet Electronics
105-2550 Boundary
Burmalay V5M 3Z3
Tel: (604) 437-6667

Zentronics
108-11400 Bridgeport Road
Richmond V6X 1T2
Tel: (604) 273-5575
TWX: 04-5077-89

MANITOBA

Zentronics
60-1313 Border Unit 60
Winnipeg R3H 0X4
Tel: (204) 694-1957

ONTARIO

Arrow Electronics, Inc.
36 Antares Dr.
Nepean K2E 7W5
Tel: (613) 226-6903

Arrow Electronics, Inc.
1093 Meyerside
Mississauga L5T 1M4
Tel: (416) 673-7769
TWX: 06-218213

†Hamilton/Avnet Electronics
6845 Rexwood Road
Units 3-4-5
Mississauga L4T 1R2
Tel: (416) 677-7432
TWX: 610-492-8867

Hamilton/Avnet Electronics
6845 Rexwood Rd., Unit 6
Mississauga L4T 1R2
Tel: (416) 277-0484

†Hamilton/Avnet Electronics
190 Colonnade Road South
Nepean K2E 7L5
Tel: (613) 226-1700
TWX: 05-349-71

†Zentronics
8 Tilbury Court
Brampton L6T 3T4
Tel: (416) 451-9600
TWX: 06-976-78

†Zentronics
155 Colonnade Road
Unit 17
Nepean K2E 7K1
Tel: (613) 226-8840

Zentronics
60-1313 Border St.
Winnipeg R3H 0I4
Tel: (204) 694-7957

QUEBEC

†Arrow Electronics Inc.
4050 Jean Talon Quest
Montreal H4P 1W1
Tel: (514) 735-5511
TWX: 05-25590

Arrow Electronics, Inc.
500 Avenue St-Jean Baptiste
Suite 280
Quebec G2E 5R9
Tel: (418) 871-7500
FAX: 418-871-6816

Hamilton/Avnet Electronics
2795 Halpern
St. Laurent H2E 7K1
Tel: (514) 335-1000
TWX: 610-421-3731

Zentronics
817 McCaffrey
St. Laurent H4T 1M3
Tel: (514) 737-9700
TWX: 05-827-535

†Microcomputer System Technical Distributor Center

EUROPEAN SALES OFFICES

DENMARK

Intel Denmark A/S
Glentevej 61, 3rd Floor
2400 Copenhagen NV
Tel: (45) (31) 19 80 33
TLX: 19567

FINLAND

Intel Finland OY
Ruosilantie 2
00390 Helsinki
Tel: (358) 0 544 644
TLX: 123332

FRANCE

Intel Corporation S.A.R.L.
1, Rue Edison-BP 303
78054 St. Quentin-en-Yvelines
Cedex
Tel: (33) (1) 30 57 70 00
TLX: 699016

WEST GERMANY

Intel Semiconductor GmbH*
Dornacher Strasse 1
8016 Feldkirchen bei Muenchen
Tel: (49) 089/90992-0
TLX: 5-23177
FAX: 904-3948

Intel Semiconductor GmbH
Hohenzollern Strasse 5
3000 Hannover 1
Tel: (49) 0511/344081
TLX: 9-23625

Intel Semiconductor GmbH
Abraham Lincoln Strasse 16-18
6200 Wiesbaden
Tel: (49) 06121/7605-0
TLX: 4-186183

Intel Semiconductor GmbH
Zettachring 10A
7000 Stuttgart 80
Tel: (49) 0711/7287-280
TLX: 7-254826

ISRAEL

Intel Semiconductor Ltd.*
Atidim Industrial Park-Neve Sharet
P.O. Box 43202
Tel-Aviv 61430
Tel: (972) 03-498080
TLX: 371215

ITALY

Intel Corporation Italia S.p.A.*
Milanofiori Palazzo E
20090 Assago
Milano
Tel: (39) (02) 89200950
TLX: 341286

NETHERLANDS

Intel Semiconductor B.V.*
Postbus 84130
3099 CC Rotterdam
Tel: (31) 10.407.11.11
TLX: 22283

NORWAY

Intel Norway A/S
Hvamveien 4-PO Box 92
2013 Skjetten
Tel: (47) (6) 842 420
TLX: 78018

SPAIN

Intel Iberia S.A.
Zurbaran, 28
28010 Madrid
Tel: (34) 308.25.52
TLX: 46880

SWEDEN

Intel Sweden A.B.*
Dalvagen 24
171 36 Solna
Tel: (46) 8 734 01 00
TLX: 12261

SWITZERLAND

Intel Semiconductor A.G.
Zuerichstrasse
8185 Winkel-Rueti bei Zuerich
Tel: (41) 01/860 62 62
TLX: 825977

UNITED KINGDOM

Intel Corporation (U.K.) Ltd.*
Pipers Way
Swindon, Wiltshire SN3 1RJ
Tel: (44) (0793) 696000
TLX: 444447/8

EUROPEAN DISTRIBUTORS/REPRESENTATIVES

AUSTRIA

Bacher Electronics G.m.b.H.
Rotenmuehlgasse 26
1120 Wien
Tel: (43) (0222) 83 56 46
TLX: 31532

BELGIUM

Inelco Belgium S.A.
Av. des Croix de Guerre 94
1120 Bruxelles
Oorlogskruisenlaan, 94
1120 Brussel
Tel: (32) (02) 216 01 60
TLX: 64475 or 22090

DENMARK

ITT-Multikomponent
Naverland 29
2600 Glostrup
Tel: (45) (0) 2 45 66 45
TLX: 33 355

FINLAND

OY Fintronic AB
Melkonkatu 24A
00210 Helsinki
Tel: (358) (0) 6926022
TLX: 124224

FRANCE

Almex
Zone industrielle d'Antony
48, rue de l'Aubepine
BP 102
92164 Antony cedex
Tel: (33) (1) 46 66 21 12
TLX: 250067

Jermyn-Generim
60, rue des Gemeaux
Silic 580
94653 Rungis cedex
Tel: (33) (1) 49 78 49 78
TLX: 260967

Metrologie
Tour d'Asnieres
4, av. Laurent-Cely
92606 Asnieres Cedex
Tel: (33) (1) 47 90 62 40
TLX: 611448

Tekelec-Airtronic
Cite des Bruyeres
Rue Carle Vernet - BP 2
92310 Sevres
Tel: (33) (1) 45 34 75 35
TLX: 204552

WEST GERMANY

Electronic 2000 AG
Stahlgruberring 12
8000 Muenchen 82
Tel: (49) 089/42001-0
TLX: 522561

ITT Multikomponent GmbH
Postfach 1265
Bahnhofstrasse 44
7141 Moeglingen
Tel: (49) 07141/4879
TLX: 7264472

Jermyn GmbH
Im Dachsstueck 9
6250 Limburg
Tel: (49) 06431/508-0
TLX: 415257-0

Metrologie GmbH
Meglingerstrasse 49
8000 Muenchen 71
Tel: (49) 089/78042-0
TLX: 5213189

Proelectron Vertriebs GmbH
Max Planck Strasse 1-3
6072 Dreieich
Tel: (49) 06103/30434-3
TLX: 417903

IRELAND

Micro Marketing Ltd.
Glenageary Office Park
Glenageary
Co. Dublin
Tel: (21) (353) (01) 85 63 25
TLX: 31584

ISRAEL

Eastronics Ltd.
11 Rozanis Street
P.O.B. 39300
Tel-Aviv 61392
Tel: (972) 03-475151
TLX: 33638

ITALY

Intesi
Divisione ITT Industries GmbH
Viale Milanofiori
Palazzo E/5
20090 Assago (MI)
Tel: (39) 02/824701
TLX: 311351

Lasi Elettronica S.p.A.
V. le Fulvio Testi, 126
20092 Cinisello Balsamo (MI)
Tel: (39) 02/2440012
TLX: 352040

ITT Multicomponents
Viale Milanofiori E/5
20090 Assago (MI)
Tel: (39) 02/824701
TLX: 311351

Silverstar
Via Dei Gracchi 20
20146 Milano
Tel: (39) 02/49961
TLX: 332189

NETHERLANDS

Koning en Hartman Elektrotechniek
B.V.
Energieweg 1
2627 AP Delft
Tel: (31) (0) 15/609906
TLX: 38250

NORWAY

Nordisk Elektronikk (Norge) A/S
Postboks 123
Smedsvingen 4
1364 Hvalstad
Tel: (47) (02) 84 62 10
TLX: 77546

PORTUGAL

ATD Portugal
Rua Dos Lusiadas, 5 Sala B
1300 LISBOA
Tel: 64 80 91
TLX: 61562
FAX: 63 76 55

Ditram
Avenida Miguel Bombarda, 133
1000 Lisboa
Tel: (35) (1) 734 884
TLX: 14182

SPAIN

ATD Electronica, S.A.
Plaza Ciudad de Viena, 6
28040 Madrid
Tel: (34) (1) 234 40 00
TLX: 42754

ITT-SESA
Calle Miguel Angel, 21-3
28010 Madrid
Tel: (34) (1) 419 54 00
TLX: 27461

Metrologia Iberica, S.A.
Ctra. de Fuencarral, n.80
28100 Alcobendas (Madrid)
Tel: (34) (1) 653 86 11

SWEDEN

Nordisk Elektronik AB
Huvudstagatan 1
Box 1409
171 27 Solna
Tel: (46) 08-734 97 70
TLX: 105 47

SWITZERLAND

Industrade A.G.
Hertistrasse 31
8304 Wallisellen
Tel: (41) (01) 8328111
TLX: 56788

TURKEY

EMPA Electronic
Lindwurmstrasse 95A
8000 Muenchen 2
Tel: (49) 089/53 80 570
TLX: 528573

UNITED KINGDOM

Accent Electronic Components Ltd.
Jubilee House, Jubilee Road
Letchworth, Herts SG6 1TL
Tel: (44) (0462) 686666
TLX: 826293

Bytech-Comway Systems
3 The Western Centre
Western Road
Bracknell RG12 1RW
Tel: (44) (0344) 55333
TLX: 847201

Jermyn
Vestry Estate
Otford Road
Sevenoaks
Kent TN14 5EU
Tel: (44) (0732) 450144
TLX: 95142

MMD
Unit 8 Southview Park
Caversham
Reading
Berkshire RG4 0AF
Tel: (44) (0734) 481666
TLX: 846669

Rapid Silicon
Rapid House
Denmark Street
High Wycombe
Buckinghamshire HP11 2ER
Tel: (44) (0494) 442266
TLX: 837931

Rapid Systems
Rapid House
Denmark Street
High Wycombe
Buckinghamshire HP11 2ER
Tel: (44) (0494) 450244
TLX: 837931

YUGOSLAVIA

H.R. Microelectronics Corp.
2005 de la Cruz Blvd., Ste. 223
Santa Clara, CA 95050
U.S.A.
Tel: (1) (408) 988-0286
TLX: 387452

Rapido Electronic Components
S.p.a.
Via C. Beccaria, 8
34133 Trieste
Italia
Tel: (39) 040/360555
TLX: 460461

*Field Application Location

INTERNATIONAL SALES OFFICES

AUSTRALIA

Intel Australia Pty. Ltd.*
Spectrum Building
200 Pacific Hwy., Level 6
Crows Nest, NSE, 2065
Tel: 612-957-2744
FAX: 612-923-2632

BRAZIL

Intel Semicondutores do Brazil LTDA
Av. Paulista, 1159-CJS 404/405
01311 - Sao Paulo - S.P.
Tel: 55-11-287-5899
TLX: 3911153146 ISDB
FAX: 55-11-287-5899

CHINA/HONG KONG

Intel PRC Corporation
15/F, Office 1, Citic Bldg.
Jian Guo Men Wai Street
Beijing, PRC
Tel: (1) 500-4850
TLX: 22947 INTEL CN
FAX: (1) 500-2953

Intel Semiconductor Ltd.*
10/F East Tower
Bond Center
Queensway, Central
Hong Kong
Tel: (5) 8444-555
TLX: 63869 ISHLHK HX
FAX: (5) 8681-989

INDIA

Intel Asia Electronics, Inc.
4/2, Samrah Plaza
St. Mark's Road
Bangalore 560001
Tel: 011-91-812-215065
TLX: 9538452875 DCBY
FAX: 091-812-563982

JAPAN

Intel Japan K.K.
5-6 Tokodai, Tsukuba-shi
Ibaraki, 300-26
Tel: 029747-8511
TLX: 3656-160
FAX: 029747-8450

Intel Japan K.K.*
Daiichi Mitsugi Bldg.
1-8889 Fuchu-cho
Fuchu-shi, Tokyo 183
Tel: 0423-60-7871
FAX: 0423-60-0315

Intel Japan K.K.*
Flower-Hill Shin-machi Bldg.
1-23-9 Shinmachi
Setagaya-ku, Tokyo 154
Tel: 03-426-2231
FAX: 03-427-7620

Intel Japan K.K.*
Bldg. Kumagaya
2-69 Hon-cho
Kumagaya-shi, Saitama 360
Tel: 0485-24-6871
FAX: 0485-24-7518

Intel Japan K.K.*
Mitsui-Seimei Musashi-kosugi Bldg.
915 Shinmaruko, Nakahara-ku
Kawasaki-shi, Kanagawa 211
Tel: 044-733-7011
FAX: 044-733-7010

Intel Japan K.K.
Nihon Seimei Atsugi Bldg.
1-2-1 Asahi-machi
Atsugi-shi, Kanagawa 243
Tel: 0462-29-3731
FAX: 0462-29-3781

Intel Japan K.K.*
Ryokuchi-Eki Bldg.
2-4-1 Terauchi
Toyonaka-shi, Osaka 560
Tel: 06-863-1091
FAX: 06-863-1084

Intel Japan K.K.
Shinmaru Bldg.
1-5-1 Marunouchi
Chiyoda-ku, Tokyo 100
Tel: 03-201-3621
FAX: 03-201-6850

Intel Japan K.K.
Green Bldg.
1-16-20 Nishiki
Naka-ku, Nagoya-shi
Aichi 450
Tel: 052-204-1261
FAX: 052-204-1285

KOREA

Intel Technology Asia, Ltd.
16th Floor, Life Bldg.
61 Yoido-Dong, Youngdeungpo-Ku
Seoul 150-010
Tel: (2) 784-8186, 8286, 8386
TLX: K29312 INTELKO
FAX: (2) 784-8096

SINGAPORE

Intel Singapore Technology, Ltd.
101 Thomson Road #21-05/06
United Square
Singapore 1130
Tel: 250-7811
TLX: 39921 INTEL
FAX: 250-9256

TAIWAN

Intel Technology Far East Ltd.
8th Floor, No. 205
Bank Tower Bldg.
Tung Hua N. Road
Taipei
Tel: 886-2-716-9660
TLX: 13159 INTELTWN
FAX: 886-2-717-2455

INTERNATIONAL DISTRIBUTORS/REPRESENTATIVES

ARGENTINA

DAFSYS S.R.L.
Chacabuco, 90-6 PISO
1069-Buenos Aires
Tel: 54-1-334-7726
FAX: 54-1-334-1871

AUSTRALIA

Email Electronics
15-17 Hume Street
Huntingdale, 3166
Tel: 011-61-3-544-8244
TLX: AA 30895
FAX: 011-61-3-543-8179

NSD-Australia
205 Middle Brough Rd.
Box Hill, Victoria 3128
Tel: 03 8900970
FAX: 03 8990819

BRAZIL

Elebra Microelectronica S.A.
Rua Geraldo Flausina Gomes, 78
10th Floor
04575 - Sao Paulo - S.P.
Tel: 55-11-534-9641
TLX: 55-11-54593/54591
FAX: 55-11-534-9424

CHILE

DIN Instruments
Suecia 2323
Casilla 6055, Correo 22
Santiago
Tel: 56-2-225-8139
TLX: 240.846 RUD

CHINA/HONG KONG

Novel Precision Machinery Co., Ltd.
Flat D, 20 Kingsford Ind. Bldg.
Phase 1, 26 Kwai Hei Street
N.T., Kowloon
Hong Kong
Tel: 852-0-4223222
TWX: 39114 JINMI HX
FAX: 852-0-4261602

INDIA

Micronic Devices
Arun Complex
No. 65 D.V.G. Road
Basavanagudi
Bangalore 560 004
Tel: 011-91-812-600-631
011-91-812-621-455
TLX: 9538458332 MDBG

Micronic Devices
Flat 403, Gagan Deep
12, Rajendra Place
New Delhi 110 008
Tel: 011-91-11-589771
TLX: 9533163235 MDND

Micronic Devices
No. 516 5th Floor
Swastik Chambers
Sion, Trombay Road
Chembur
Bombay 400 071
TLX: 9531 171447 MDEV

S&S Corporation
Camden Business Center
Suite 6
1610 Blossom Hill Rd.
San Jose, CA 95124
U.S.A.
Tel: (408) 978-6216
TLX: 820281

JAPAN

Asahi Electronics Co. Ltd.
KMM Bldg. 2-14-1 Asano
Kokurakita-ku
Kitakyushu-shi 802
Tel: 093-511-6471
FAX: 093-551-7861

C. Itoh Techno-Science Co., Ltd.
4-8-1 Dobashi, Miyamae-ku
Kawasaki-shi, Kanagawa 213
Tel: 044-852-5121
FAX: 044-877-4268

Dia Semicon Systems, Inc.
Wacore 64, 1-37-8 Sangenjaya
Setagaya-ku, Tokyo 154
Tel: 03-487-0386
FAX: 03-487-8088

Okaya Koki
2-4-18 Sakae
Naka-ku, Nagoya-shi 460
Tel: 052-204-2916
FAX: 052-204-2901

Ryoyo Electro Corp.
Konwa Bldg.
1-12-22 Tsukiji
Chuo-ku, Tokyo 104
Tel: 03-546-5011
FAX: 03-546-5044

KOREA

J-Tek Corporation
6th Floor, Government Pension Bldg.
24-3 Yoido-Dong
Youngdeungpo-ku
Seoul 150-010
Tel: 82-2-780-8039
TLX: 25299 KODIGIT
FAX: 82-2-784-8391

Samsung Semiconductor &
Telecommunications Co., Ltd.
150 Taepyungro-2 KA
Chungku, Seoul 100-102
Tel: 82-2-751-3985
TLX: 27970 KORSST
FAX: 82-2-753-0967

MEXICO

Dicopel S.A.
Av. Federalismo Sur
268-2-PLSO
C.P. 44-100-Guadalajara
Tel: 52-36-26-1232
TLX: 681663 DICOME
FAX: 52-36-26-3966

Dicopel S.A.
Tochtli 368 Fracc. Ind. San Antonio
Azcapotzalco
C.P. 02760-Mexico, D.F.
Tel: 52-5-561-3211
TLX: 1773790 DICOME
FAX: 52-5-561-1279

NEW ZEALAND

Switch Enterprises
36 Olive Road
Penrose, Auckland
Tel: 011-64-9-591155
FAX: 64-9-592681

SINGAPORE

Electronic Resources Pte. Ltd.
17 Harvey Road #03-01
Singapore 1336
Tel: 283-0888
TWX: 56541 ERS
FAX: 2895327

SOUTH AFRICA

Electronic Building Elements
178 Erasmus Street
Meyerspark, Pretoria, 0184
Tel: 011-2712-803-7680
FAX: 011-2712-803-8290

TAIWAN

Micro Electronics Corporation
5/F 587, Ming Shen East Rd.
Taipei, R.O.C.
Tel: 886-2-501-8231
FAX: 886-2-501-4265

Sertek
7/F 135, Section 2
Chien Juo North Rd.
Taipei 10479
R.O.C.
Tel: (02) 5010055
FAX: (02) 5012521
(02) 5058414

VENEZUELA

P. Benavides S.A.
Avilanes a Rio
Residencia Kamarata
Locales 4 AL 7
La Candelaria, Caracas
Tel: 58-2-574-6338
TLX: 28450
FAX: 58-2-572-3321

*Field Application Location

DOMESTIC SERVICE OFFICES

ALABAMA

Intel Corp.*
5015 Bradford Dr., #2
Huntsville 35805
Tel: (205) 830-4010

ALASKA

c/o TransAlaska Data Systems
300 Old Steese Hwy.
Fairbanks 99701-3120
Tel: (907) 452-4401

c/o TransAlaska Data Systems
1551 Lore Road
Anchorage 99507
Tel: (907) 522-1776

ARIZONA

Intel Corp.*
11225 N. 28th Dr.
Suite D-214
Phoenix 85029
Tel: (602) 869-4980

Intel Corp.*
500 E. Fry Blvd., Suite M-15
Sierra Vista 85635
Tel: (602) 459-5010

CALIFORNIA

Intel Corp.
21515 Vanowen St., Ste. 116
Canoga Park 91303
Tel: (818) 704-8500

Intel Corp.*
2250 E. Imperial Hwy., Ste. 218
El Segundo 90245
Tel: (213) 640-6040

Intel Corp.*
1900 Prairie City Rd.
Folsom 95630-9597
Tel: (916) 351-6143
1-800-468-3548

Intel Corp.**
400 N. Tustin Avenue
Suite 450
Santa Ana 92705
Tel: (714) 835-9642

Intel Corp.**
San Tomas 4
2700 San Tomas Exp., 2nd Floor
Santa Clara 95051
Tel: (408) 986-8086

COLORADO

Intel Corp.*
650 S. Cherry St., Suite 915
Denver 80222
Tel: (303) 321-8086

CONNECTICUT

Intel Corp.*
26 Mill Plain Road
2nd Floor
Danbury 06811
Tel: (203) 748-3130
TWX: 710-456-1199

FLORIDA

Intel Corp.**
6363 N.W. 6th Way, Ste. 100
Ft. Lauderdale 33309
Tel: (305) 771-0600

Intel Corp.*
5850 T.G. Lee Blvd., Ste. 340
Orlando 32822
Tel: (407) 240-8000

GEORGIA

Intel Corp.*
3280 Pointe Pkwy., Ste. 200
Norcross 30092
Tel: (404) 449-0541

HAWAII

U.S.I.S.C. Signal Batt.*
Building T-1521
Shafter Plats
Shafter 96856

ILLINOIS

Intel Corp.**
300 N. Martingale Rd., Ste. 400
Schaumburg 60173
Tel: (312) 605-8031

INDIANA

Intel Corp.*
8777 Purdue Rd., Ste. 125
Indianapolis 46268
Tel: (317) 875-0623

KANSAS

Intel Corp.*
10985 Cody, Suite 140
Overland Park 66210
Tel: (913) 345-2727

MARYLAND

Intel Corp.**
7833 Walker Dr., 4th Floor
Greenbelt 20770
Tel: (301) 441-1020

MASSACHUSETTS

Intel Corp.**
3 Carlisle Rd., 2nd Floor
Westford 01886
Tel: (508) 692-1060

MICHIGAN

Intel Corp.*
7071 Orchard Lake Rd., Ste. 100
West Bloomfield 48322
Tel: (313) 851-8905

MINNESOTA

Intel Corp.*
3500 W. 80th St., Suite 360
Bloomington 55431
Tel: (612) 835-6722

MISSOURI

Intel Corp.*
4203 Earth City Exp., Ste. 131
Earth City 63045
Tel: (314) 291-1990

NEW JERSEY

Intel Corp.**
300 Sylvan Avenue
Englewood Cliffs 07632
Tel: (201) 567-0821
TWX: 710-991-8593

Intel Corp.*
Parkway 109 Office Center
328 Newman Springs Road
Red Bank 07701
Tel: (201) 747-2233

Intel Corp.*
280 Corporate Center
75 Livingston Ave., 1st Floor
Roseland 07068
Tel: (201) 740-0111

NEW YORK

Intel Corp.*
2950 Expressway Dr. South
Islandia 11722
Tel: (516) 231-3300

Intel Corp.*
Westage Business Center
Bldg. 300, Route 9
Fishkill 12524
Tel: (914) 897-3860

NORTH CAROLINA

Intel Corp.*
5800 Executive Dr., Ste. 105
Charlotte 28212
Tel: (704) 568-8966

Intel Corp.**
2700 Wycliff Rd., Ste. 102
Raleigh 27607
Tel: (919) 851-9537

OHIO

Intel Corp.**
3401 Park Center Dr., Ste. 220
Dayton 45414
Tel: (513) 890-5350

Intel Corp.*
25700 Science Park Dr., Ste. 100
Beachwood 44122
Tel: (216) 464-2736

OREGON

Intel Corp.
15254 N.W. Greenbrier Parkway
Building B
Beaverton 97005
Tel: (503) 645-8051

Intel Corp.*
5200 N.E. Elam Young Parkway
Hillsboro 97123
Tel: (503) 681-8080

PENNSYLVANIA

Intel Corp.*
455 Pennsylvania Ave., Ste. 230
Fort Washington 19034
Tel: (215) 641-1000

Intel Corp.
400 Penn Center Blvd., Ste. 610
Pittsburgh 15235
Tel: (412) 823-4970

Intel Corp.
1513 Cedar Cliff Dr.
Camp Hill 17011
Tel: (717) 761-0860

PUERTO RICO

Intel Microprocessor Corp.
South Industrial Park
P.O. Box 910
Las Piedras 00671
Tel: (809) 733-8616

TEXAS

Intel Corp.
8815 Dyer St., Suite 225
El Paso 79904
Tel: (915) 751-0186

Intel Corp.*
313 E. Anderson Ln., Ste. 314
Austin 78752
Tel: (512) 454-3628

Intel Corp.**
12000 Ford Rd., Suite 401
Dallas 75234
Tel: (214) 241-8087

Intel Corp.*
7322 S.W. Freeway, Ste. 1490
Houston 77074
Tel: (713) 988-8086

UTAH

Intel Corp.
428 East 6400 South, Ste. 104
Murray 84107
Tel: (801) 263-8051

VIRGINIA

Intel Corp.*
1504 Santa Rosa Rd., Ste. 108
Richmond 23288
Tel: (804) 282-5668

WASHINGTON

Intel Corp.*
155 108th Avenue N.E., St.e 386
Bellevue 98004
Tel: (206) 453-8086

CANADA

ONTARIO

Intel Semiconductor of Canada, Ltd.
2650 Queensview Dr., Ste. 250
Ottawa K2B 8H6
Tel: (613) 829-9714
FAX: 613-820-5936

Intel Semiconductor of Canada, Ltd.
190 Attwell Dr., Ste. 102
Rexdale M9W 6HB
Tel: (416) 675-2105

CUSTOMER TRAINING CENTERS

CALIFORNIA

2700 San Tomas Expressway
Santa Clara 95051
Tel: (408) 970-1700

ILLINOIS

300 N. Martingale, #300
Schaumburg 60173
Tel: (312) 310-5700

MASSACHUSETTS

3 Carlisle Road
Westford 01886
Tel: (508) 692-1000

MARYLAND

7833 Walker Dr., 4th Floor
Greenbelt 20770
Tel: (301) 220-3380

SYSTEMS ENGINEERING OFFICES

CALIFORNIA

2700 San Tomas Expressway
Santa Clara 95051
Tel: (408) 986-8086

ILLINOIS

300 N. Martingale, #300
Schaumburg 60173
Tel: (312) 310-8031

NEW YORK

300 Motor Parkway
Hauppauge 11788
Tel: (516) 231-3300

*Carry-in locations
**Carry-in/mail-in locations